REMEMBERING GUY LAFLEUR

REMEMBERING GUY LAFLEUR

A CELEBRATION

CRAIG MacINNIS, EDITOR

RAINCOAST BOOKS

Vancouver

Raincoast Books gratefully acknowledges the ongoing support of the Canada Council for the Arts; the British Columbia Arts Council; and the Government of Canada through the Department of Canadian Heritage Book Publishing Industry Development Program (BPIDP).

Raincoast Books
9050 Shaughnessy Street
Vancouver, British Columbia
Canada V6P 6E5
www.raincoast.com

In the United States:
Publishers Group West
1700 Fourth Street
Berkeley, California
USA 94710

Library of Congress Control Number: 2004092414

National Library of Canada Cataloguing in Publication

Remembering Guy Lafleur / Craig MacInnis, editor.

ISBN 1-55192-701-2 (bound)

1. Lafleur, Guy, 1951- 2. Hockey players--Quebec (Province)--Biography. I. MacInnis, Craig

GV848.5.L34M33 2004   796.962'092   C2004-901780-2

Printed and bound in Canada.

1 2 3 4 5 6 7 8 9 10

ART DIRECTION AND DESIGN: BILL DOUGLAS AT THE BANG

For photo credits, see p. 114

CONTENTS

DEM BLUES: LAFLEUR ATTACKS
THE ST. LOUIS ZONE.

PORTRAIT
OF THE ARTIST
AS A YOUNG SCORING
MACHINE

THE ETERNAL CANADIEN
BY CRAIG MacINNIS

IT'S NO SECRET that many of hockey's best players have also been superior athletes, fine physical specimens like Bobby Hull, Jean Beliveau, Tim Horton. Equally successful are the wiry, high-energy types exemplified by Wayne Gretzky, whose sharp reflexes and sled-dog stamina were matched by his intuition with the puck. Gretzky rewrote the record books, but in some ways his skills were conventional — ordinary talents in puck-handling, passing and shooting, but so finely honed that they came to seem superhuman.

Much rarer are the "artists," players whose affinity for the game seems to emerge less from their physical attributes than from their sense of the rink as a blank canvas on which to daub their abstract expressionist vision.

As such, they are frequently misunderstood and often scorned by coaches who expect them to submit to a "system," to blend into a unified game plan. They are also worshipped by their adoring fans, for their game is not the game of plugging and striving but a game that seeks redemption through a state of near metaphysical grace. (That sound you just heard was Don Cherry slamming the cover of this book shut.)

Guy Lafleur, the Montreal Canadiens' great right-winger, was an artist. So was his Habs predecessor Rocket Richard, who was more temperamental than Lafleur yet burned with the same certainty that the game's

DOUBLE TROUBLE: LAFLEUR,
THE ATHLETE AS ARTIST.

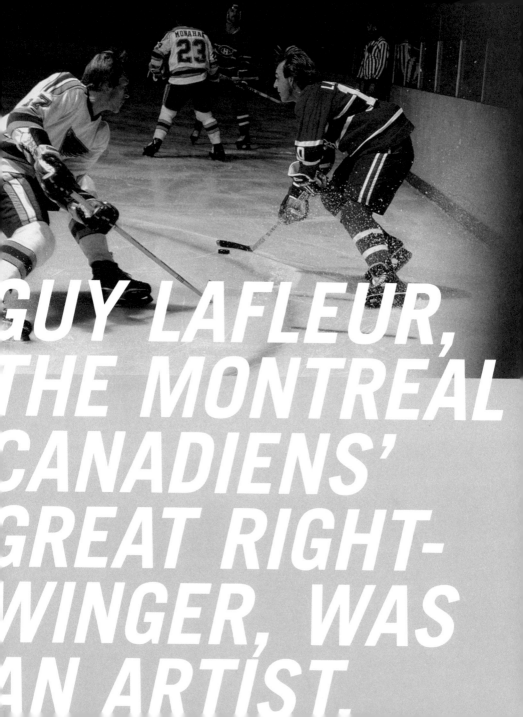

GUY LAFLEUR, THE MONTREAL CANADIENS' GREAT RIGHT-WINGER, WAS AN ARTIST.

course followed the exact cut of his skate blades, the precise trajectory of his shot. What about Beliveau? Beliveau was superb, but Beliveau was too upstanding, too of-the-team, to venture into that chancy realm where Lafleur and Richard found greatness. In the best sense of the words, Beliveau was the Habs' "company man," while Richard and Lafleur were insurrectionists, willing to embrace chaos, willing to stand alone.

Both performed with a fiery, nonconformist zeal that often defied their team's strategies. In fact, with Richard or Lafleur in your lineup you didn't need a game plan. Just let them on the ice and watch art triumph over the opposition's futile mathematics.

In hindsight, Lafleur's and Richard's artistry was the fulcrum on which their legends teetered. It made them great, but it also sent them down toward the abyss, the dark void where corporate planning trumps art every time. It is no coincidence that both men felt spurned by the team to which they had lashed their souls, and that their leave-taking — Richard's in September 1960, Lafleur's in November 1984 — made for unprecedented hand-wringing in the province of Quebec.

In his waning days in Montreal, Lafleur was benched for long stretches and fell afoul of his coach, Jacques Lemaire, his old friend and linemate, who seemed determined to turn Lafleur into an efficient two-way player.

"There's an adaptation you have to make when you get older," said Lemaire. "You need more set patterns and areas in order to give the other guys the chance to get the puck, but Guy never worked like that. Maybe he could never do it because he had always been so natural."

Lemaire, who never guided a team from which he couldn't erase every nuance of offensive zest (Montreal, New Jersey, Minnesota), would win a Cup

03

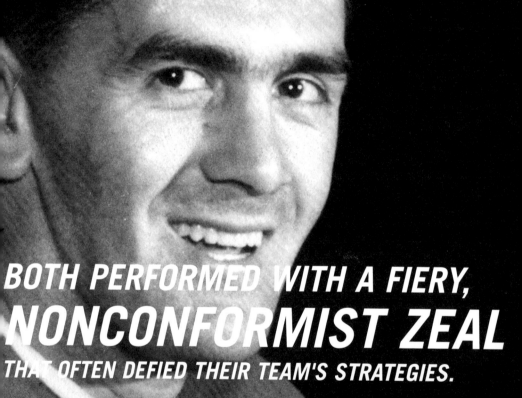

BOTH PERFORMED WITH A FIERY, NONCONFORMIST ZEAL
THAT OFTEN DEFIED THEIR TEAM'S STRATEGIES.

ARTISTIC TEMPERAMENTS — HABS GREAT
ROCKET RICHARD AND HIS STYLISTIC HEIR.

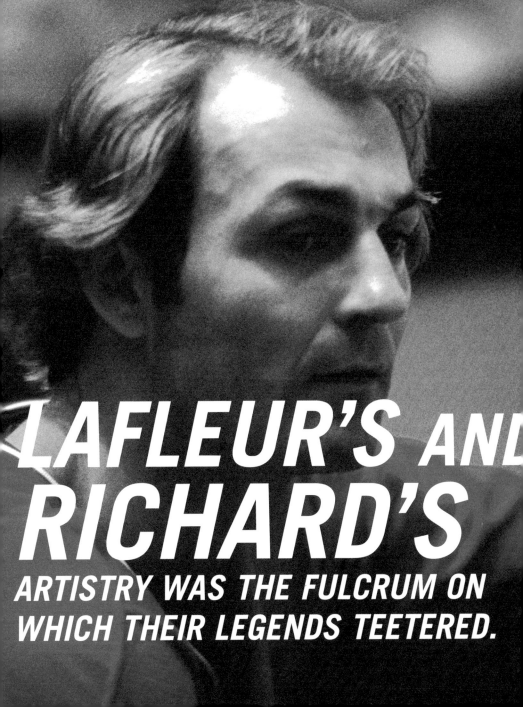

LAFLEUR'S AND RICHARD'S

ARTISTRY WAS THE FULCRUM ON WHICH THEIR LEGENDS TEETERED.

with the Devils in 1995, but never won the admiration of purists. He is an adherent of the neutral-zone trap, a defensive system that depends on breaking up the flow of a play before it begins, which is the temperamental and strategic opposite of what Lafleur stood for.

IN 1987, LAFLEUR WOULD INTERRUPT HIS RETIREMENT TO PLAY THREE MORE SEASONS — ONE IN NEW YORK FOR THE RANGERS AND TWO WITH QUEBEC.

But it doesn't really matter that "the Flower" (as he was known to his English-speaking fans), finished his career in enemy colours. Like Richard, he will always be the Eternal Canadien, a player who not only defined an era but whose hockey-related travails were seen by some as religious allegory.

When Lafleur retired from the Habs, Bertrand Raymond, sports editor of *Le Journal*, Montreal's sporting bible, compared his burden to the heavy load carried by "Christ to Calvary."

In the *Globe and Mail*, Scott Disher perceptively likened "Ti-Guy" to then premier Rene Levesque, another flawed but beloved figure. "From the day Jean Beliveau retired in 1971, Ti-Guy's comings and goings, flashy cars and his golfing, hunting and softball exploits have been dutifully recorded and interpreted in glowing detail," wrote Disher.

"His smoking and drinking, marital problems, contracts disputes, near-fatal car crash and run-ins with game wardens have endeared him to an admiring public, perhaps more than his on-ice feats.

"Like Rene Levesque, whose future seems to be unfolding in a soap operatic fashion similar to the Flower's, Lafleur has become the universal property of all Quebeckers. If the two Jeans — Beliveau and [1960s Quebec premier

LONE RANGER: LAFLEUR, IN NEW YORK BLUE,
RETURNS TO THE FORUM.

Jean] Lesage — were vaguely suspected of playing Uncle Tom to *les Anglais* and were perceived as being a trifle too aloof and goody-goody for the common taste, Lafleur and Levesque have come to embody the wildly ambivalent feelings of at least two generations of Quebeckers."

Apart from his dazzling end-to-end displays of skill, including six straight 50-goal seasons during his 1970s heyday, Lafleur's great gift to the people of Quebec was his unbuttoned lip, his artistic temperament. No one spoke with such candour, or with such blithe disregard for protocol.

During the early weeks of 1976, controversy erupted over Lafleur's use of Koho hockey sticks, which were made in Finland. Why couldn't he use a French-Canadian stick? In Quebec, where issues of nationalism lie at the edge of every spirited hockey debate, Lafleur's stick preference was construed as a political snub. Not that Lafleur cared — he was never very political. His response to his critics was a poetic discourse on the mysteries of his game.

"The stick issue was essential for me because the capacity to 'feel' the puck adds something to my play," he told his French-language biographer, Claude Larochelle. "If I have a secret in hockey, it is very simple while at the same time kind of strange. It's difficult to believe, but I don't relax and rest up on the bench. I find my relaxation on the ice when I have that little black biscuit on the blade of my stick. Then I am motivated as if by a powerful inspiration.

"Contrary to other athletes who wear themselves out carrying the puck, I find it a way of recapturing my vitality. People are astonished at my sources of energy. They don't have to look for the reason. I know why."

He was just as engaging in the fall of 2003, when he led a team of Montreal old-timers into Edmonton to play the Oilers alumni as part of the outdoor Heritage Classic at Commonwealth Stadium.

CANADA CUP '76: LAFLEUR GOES IN
ON CZECH GOALIE VLADIMIR DZURILLA.

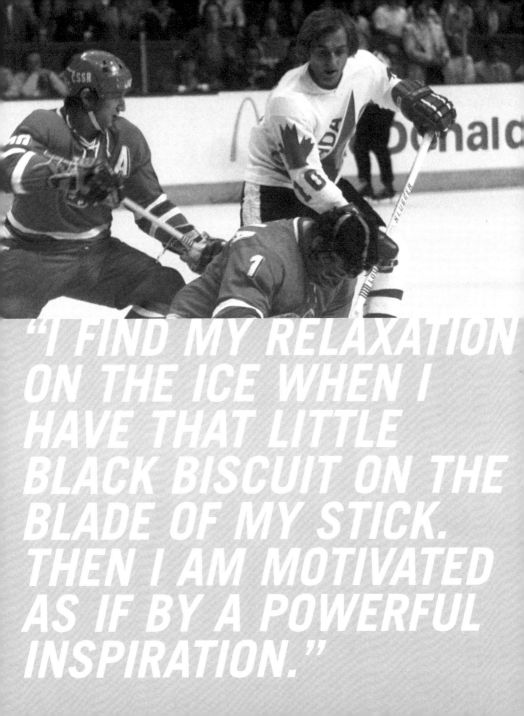

"I FIND MY RELAXATION ON THE ICE WHEN I HAVE THAT LITTLE BLACK BISCUIT ON THE BLADE OF MY STICK. THEN I AM MOTIVATED AS IF BY A POWERFUL INSPIRATION."

"Unlike today's hockey players who toil in tedium and offer up the same dreary quotes, Lafleur was aware of his status yet unafraid to speak his mind," Allan Maki wrote admiringly in the *Globe and Mail*. "If something bothered him, he let people know about it."

On this day, it was the declining state of the modern game that irked him. "Teams in the NHL today win the Stanley Cup by playing the trap," he said. "It's a good way for coaches to keep their jobs. But for the fans, I don't think it's interesting.

"You know what's the biggest problem? In the 1970s and 1980s, they spoiled the fans. Now, the game is not the same and everyone is panicking. Everyone took it for granted. People say to me, 'Your days were the best. We could identify with all the players and those days are gone.' The problem with people is they complain, complain, complain and they still go to the game."

That's because most of us, when you cut right through it, are hopeless romantics, waiting for another Lafleur to come along and blaze a new trail to greatness, to return hockey to its intended glories.

Montreal never did find another player of Lafleur's calibre. The closest was Patrick Roy, but he was a goalie, and puck-stoppers can't inflame the public's passion the way that great rushing forwards can. To alter the course of a game the way Lafleur did — routinely raising us out of our seats, inspiring us to delirium — was a special thing.

A work of art.

As the sixth subject in our series on NHL legends, Guy Lafleur embodies all of the qualities we wish for in our best players — tremendous style, staggering productivity, wildness of spirit and, above all, a gentleness with fans, the people who loved him and love him still.

In the book's closing chapter, *Montreal Gazette* sportswriter Dave Stubbs visits Lafleur at his restaurant in Berthierville, Quebec, where the ex-Hab reflects on the state of the modern game and the intricacies of menu planning.

Fellow *Gazette* writer and rock critic Mark Lepage strips away the statistics to reveal Lafleur's essential rock 'n' roll persona. Lafleur, he writes, arrived on the scene "just as the sport's image convulsed along with the culture." Lafleur would become a bigger star in Quebec than Robert Charlebois or Rene Simard, bigger even than the international touring stars who made sure to wear a Canadiens No. 10 jersey during their concerts at the Montreal Forum.

Longtime series contributor Doug Herod fondly recalls the gratitude he felt toward Lafleur when, in 1976, the Canadiens silenced Philadelphia's Broad Street Bullies in a crucial Stanley Cup clash of contrasting hockey styles.

Frank Orr, who as a beat writer for the *Toronto Star* covered Lafleur during his high-scoring heyday, weighs in with three pieces, including a primer on what made Lafleur great, a review of his greatest game, and a story outlining the horse-trading skills of former Habs GM Sam Pollock, who used his legendary wiles to pluck the Flower in the 1971 entry draft.

My own contribution is from that same year, when Lafleur's Quebec Remparts met Marcel Dionne's St. Catharines Black Hawks in a junior showdown of historic proportions. I was 14 at the time, a Black Hawk fan from the heart of English-speaking southern Ontario. By the end of the series, which sadly ended in forfeiture and name-calling, even a disgruntled 14-year-old Hawks fan could see Lafleur's greatness, could acknowledge his genius. It was simply undeniable.

A TALE
OF TWO
SOLITUDES

NO. 1 IN '71
BY CRAIG MacINNIS

WHEN 19-YEAR-OLD GUY LAFLEUR stepped onto the ice at Garden City Arena in St. Catharines on May 2, 1971, a friend and I hurried down to the end boards to watch the enemy take his pregame skate. Lafleur's Quebec Remparts had arrived in southern Ontario to do battle against our hometown St. Catharines Black Hawks, a seven-game series that would decide junior hockey supremacy in eastern Canada.

It took us about five seconds to dismiss him as a lightweight. "He looks kinda scrawny," I remember saying, feeling reassured by Lafleur's apparent wispiness. It was hard to miss the fact that he was wearing No. 4, homage to another great Quebec star, Jean Beliveau, but what could this beaky prospect possibly have in common with Beliveau?

Our skepticism was understandable. We were 14 years old. We were Black Hawks fans. Our hero was Marcel Dionne, Lafleur's arch-rival who had left his native Quebec to pursue a junior career among "the English" in the Ontario Hockey Association (OHA).

Dionne might have been thought of as a traitor by the folks back in Drummondville, where he was born, but in St. Catharines he was the toast of the town — the greatest junior star to pass through Niagara since Bobby Hull played for the St. Catharines Teepees in the mid-1950s.

13

From our perspective — which is to say, the perspective of biased, hockey-crazed teenagers — this was going to be a cakewalk for the Hawks. Who was this Lafleur, anyway, and what had he really proved with his 130 goals and 79 assists?

In the run-and-gun Quebec league, didn't they score goals by the truckload, against porous defences and goaltenders who couldn't stand upright on skates? Everyone in Ontario knew that the "Q" was a slacker league, overrun with goal-sucking prima donnas whose only acquaintance with the defensive zone was when they were forced to line up at their own blue line for the national anthem. In the OHA, the game was more disciplined and skilled, patterned to meet the demands of the NHL, which is where all the best OHA players were headed just as soon as they were drafted.

Dionne was a stickhandling marvel, a sturdy, compact dynamo who regularly weaved his way through entire teams before tapping the puck past sprawled goaltenders. His game was a bewitching amalgam of styles, as if someone had grafted the speed of an Yvan Cournoyer onto the puck-handling savvy of a Stan Mikita, then topped it with a shot that was the equal of Hull's. Not only that, but he could lay a perfect pass on a teammate's stick while looking the other way. In the regular season that year, he led the league in scoring with 62 goals and 81 assists, his second straight OHA scoring title.

No matter how one viewed it, then, the 1971 eastern Canadian Junior A hockey final — St. Catharines versus Quebec, Dionne versus Lafleur — would not only be a clash of opposing hockey cultures but a showcase of the putative No. 1 and No. 2 choices in that year's June draft. In a nifty sidebar, Maurice Filion, the Remparts' coach, had previously coached Dionne in Drummondville and seemed set on getting even for Dionne's defection to Ontario.

NIFTY MOVES: DIONNE EVADES A CHECKER.

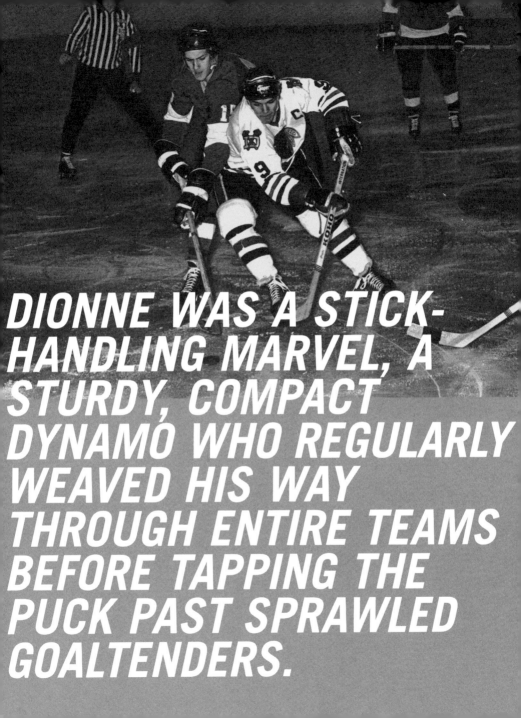

DIONNE WAS A STICK-HANDLING MARVEL, A STURDY, COMPACT DYNAMO WHO REGULARLY WEAVED HIS WAY THROUGH ENTIRE TEAMS BEFORE TAPPING THE PUCK PAST SPRAWLED GOALTENDERS.

Claude Larochelle, sports columnist for Quebec's *Le Soleil*, recalled in his book *Guy Lafleur: Hockey's #1* that Dionne's departure from Drummondville was "consummated in the midst of a barrage of insults" and that Filion had told Dionne, "Go to Ontario, Dionne. One day I'll beat you with a team from Quebec."

Arriving in St. Catharines, Filion announced to the English-speaking media that Lafleur was "the greatest junior player in the country," a comment more notable for what it implied, namely, that Dionne wasn't.

If Quebec won the series, it seemed likely that Lafleur would go first in the draft (to Montreal, who had finagled the top pick away from the hapless California Golden Seals), but if the Hawks won, everyone in St. Catharines felt certain that Dionne, with his OHA pedigree, would force the Habs to make him their first choice.

We took our seats for Game 1 and waited for the massacre to commence. Alas, it was not to be. Despite outshooting the Remparts 48 to 30, St. Catharines came out on the losing end of a 4-2 score. Dionne tallied once in the first period but played an unexceptional game.

Lafleur's teammmate (and future NHLer) Jacques Richard was the star of the night with his dazzling end-to-end rushes, but it was Lafleur who sank the Hawks with his deceptive, up-from-nowhere attack. He notched two goals, including the winner in the third period on a tap-in, but it was his first goal, at the start of the second period, that caused 3,000 St. Catharines skeptics to squirm uncomfortably in their seats.

Sportswriter Jack Gatecliff wrote about the goal in his column the next day in the *St. Catharines Standard*: "Lafleur, who plays in an almost lethargic manner until he has possession of the puck, took Michel Briere's pass just over

16

the blue line, then lashed a rocket-like shot which had such momentum that it cracked [Hawks goaltender George] Hulme's stick, then caromed into the net just under the crossbar."

I remember the silence in Garden City Arena after that shot. It was deafening. It was the silence of incomprehension, of a partisan crowd coming to terms with the terrible power unleashed by the enemy. It was a slapshot that said: Maybe those 130 goals weren't such a fluke after all.

Following the game, Filion had reason to crow: "I know Dionne is dangerous around the net but Lafleur is an all-round player. Tonight he was concentrating more on checking and didn't drive in on goal as usual."

Checking? None of us remembered that part of Lafleur's game, but we had seen enough to know he was the real deal any time he crossed the Hawks' blue line.

George Hulme, who would go on to a pro career in Detroit's minor league system, remembers Lafleur as one in a long line of great Quebec junior stars from the era. Hulme also faced the Montreal Junior Canadiens unit of Gilbert Perreault, Marc Tardif and Rejean Houle, a troika that could undress any goaltender with their intricate passing and firewagon speed. Richard Martin was another member of that junior Habs team, a preternatural sniper known to score from the other side of centre, so true and terrifying was his shot.

By Hulme's estimate, Lafleur's slapper was the hardest. "I'll never forget the way he could fire the puck. I think in Quebec City he blew one by me from the blue line," the goaltender, now in his early fifties, recalled with a smile.

"It was fast, a 'hot' shot, but it was heavy, too. Any time he came down

the wing, whether he was at his blue line or the centre-ice line, you had to be ready, because he could fire it from anywhere and there was a lot of velocity on it."

The great players, of course, never do anything according to the instruction manuals. As a junior in Oshawa, Bobby Orr knew how to shoot hard and low to the corners without seeming to "wind up." Phil Esposito could elude checks with his deft stickhandling — while standing still. Mario Lemieux created open ice for himself not by speeding up but by slowing the tempo of the game. Lafleur, whose greatness would soon be seen by a generation of *Hockey Night in Canada* fans, showed against St. Catharines that a slapshot could be "quick" and "heavy" at once.

"Most great shooters are either one or the other," muses Hulme. "You get guys with the fast but lighter shots and then the ones that blow it past you as if it's just come out of a cannon. Lafleur's shot was both of those things."

Yet all these years later Hulme still waves the flag for his old teammate, Dionne, who he feels was the "more complete player."

"Guy Lafleur, to me, was someone you had to feed the puck to and then he could score, but Marcel could take it from behind his own net and go through a whole team," says Hulme. "In my opinion, the Canadiens would have been just as well off if not better off (by drafting) Marcel, but I think he kind of got snubbed a little bit because he left Quebec to play in Ontario."

Against the Remparts, Dionne acquitted himself admirably in Game 2, notching four goals and leading the Black Hawks to an 8-3 win to tie the series at one game apiece. Lafleur was held off the scoresheet. For St. Catharines fans, the universe was unfolding as it should. Little did we know what was in store as the series shifted to the Quebec Colisée for Games 3 and 4.

ANTICIPATION: ST. CATHARINES FANS
LINE UP FOR TICKETS TO GAME 1.

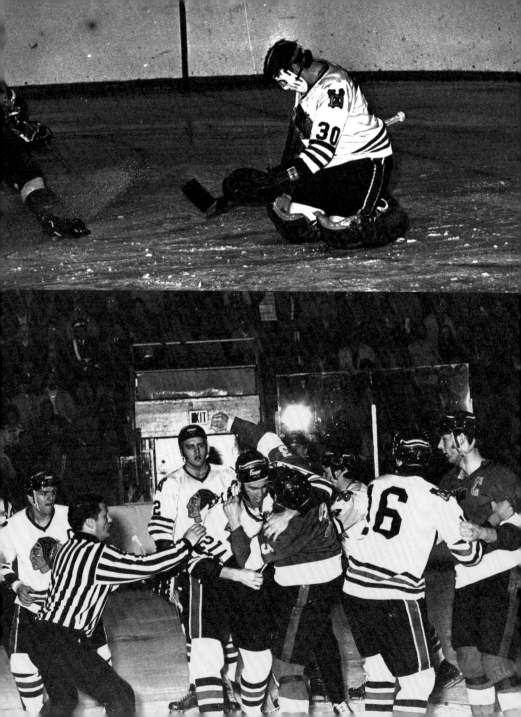

In the spring of 1971, Canada was less than a year removed from the politically divisive events of October 1970, when two separate cells of a revolutionary movement, Front de Libération du Québec (FLQ), kidnapped British trade commissioner James Cross and Quebec's labour minister, Pierre Laporte. Laporte was later found dead in the trunk of a car, while Cross' release was negotiated after his kidnappers were allowed to seek exile in Cuba.

Prime Minister Pierre Trudeau's invocation of the War Measures Act, with its suspension of civil liberties in Quebec, split the country along cultural and political lines. Quebec seemed a province alone, defensive and bruised by the federal muscle Trudeau had flexed in quelling the "apprehended insurrection."

Whether this had any material connection to the regrettable events that transpired at the Colisée in May 1971 is impossible to say. However, it's certain that the October Crisis was still too close for comfort, and that hockey has always been a flashpoint in Quebec. Sixteen years earlier, Montrealers had rioted in the streets, smashing store windows, toppling phone booths and hurling firebombs to protest NHL president Clarence Campbell's suspension of Rocket Richard from the 1955 playoffs for a stick-swinging incident in Boston.

As novelist Hugh MacLennan wrote in his famous 1955 essay in *Saturday Night* magazine, Richard "has a status with some people in Quebec not much below that of a tribal god, and I doubt if even he realizes how much of what he stands for in the public mind is only indirectly connected with the game he plays."

In Quebec City, the teenaged Lafleur was not quite an icon to match Richard, but he and his Remparts were revered. Ostentatiously, Lafleur drove

TOP: HAWKS GOALIE GEORGE HULME.
BOTTOM: LAFLEUR, FAR RIGHT, TANGLES
WITH HAWK CLYDE SIMON.

around town in a wine-red Buick Riviera, one of the perks of his $20,000 contract, an unheard-of amount for a junior in that era.

Journalist Claude Larochelle wrote about the excitement surrounding Game 3 in Quebec, where 13,896 partisans packed Le Colisée "like sardines." Hulme recalls "5,000 or 6,000 Quebec fans showing up just to watch our first practice."

Game 3 ended in a 3-1 decision for Quebec, with Lafleur scoring twice. Dionne drew an assist on the only St. Catharines goal. The Hawks directed 47 shots at the Quebec net but were held in check by the brilliant netminding of Michel Deguise. Deguise had been lent to the Remparts for the eastern Canadian finals by his home club, the Sorel Black Hawks. To obtain him Quebec used a "ringer clause," legal under Canadian Amateur Hockey Association (CAHA) rules, which enabled the league's winning team to pick up a goaltender from another club. "Deguise was really great in that series," says Hulme. "In Game 3, he was the difference."

From a hockey standpoint, Game 4 was, in Larochelle's words, "the Guy Lafleur Show." The Thurso native scored three times to lead his team in a 6-1 romp over the Hawks to take a 3-1 stranglehold on the series. Unfortunately, the stories in the next day's newspapers had little to do with the actual contest. "It was supposed to be a hockey game. All it did was make a farce of the sport," Gary McCarthy wrote in the *Montreal Gazette*. "What the crowd of 13,410 was treated to was an incredible spectacle that involved St. Catharines players, some fans and city police."

According to McCarthy, when the Hawks fell behind 6-1 in the third period "they started to lay on the muscle, giving referee Jack Bowman [Scotty's brother] fits." Bowman handed out six game misconduct penalties in

22

the last five minutes as St. Catharines players twice left the penalty box to become involved in scraps.

The worst was yet to come. When a spectator spat on Hawks player Mike Bloom as the team was heading to its dressing room, Bloom replied by "blindly swinging his stick in windmill fashion," according to Larochelle. The stick cut a police officer, Constable Yves Crete, who required three stitches above his right eye. Trying to prevent a full-scale riot, city police ushered the visiting team through a rear door of the arena, with a mob of angry Quebec fans in hot pursuit. A tire at the rear of the St. Catharines bus was slashed and a five-car police detail escorted the vehicle to the Hawks' hotel on the outskirts of the city.

Filion accused the visitors of trying to hurt his star player. "They're a disgrace to hockey," the Quebec coach said. "Why try to injure players when they're on the doorstep of a pro career? Have you noticed that none of my players have gone out of their way to hurt Dionne? Why should we? It's a good thing that Lafleur has a lot of strength and can take most of the punishment they give him. Otherwise he would have been killed out there."

To a 14-year-old listening to the game on radio back in St. Catharines — a partisan broadcast, to be sure — the story was somewhat different. So were the local newspaper accounts. "The scene inside the 20-year-old building was more like the Roman Coliseum 2,000 years ago than 20th Century Canada," Jack Gatecliff wrote in the *Standard*. "The Hawks were defeated 6-1 but the result was almost incidental to the incredible mob violence in which many of the 13,410 people who purchased tickets as spectators became active participants."

Gatecliff went further, accusing the crowd of directing most of its wrath

Phone 735-5254
WELLAND

Catharines fans behind the
bench were struck in-
ble times by spectators
g debris at the visiting
and when the game en-
icers on duty on that side
ink instructed the Hawk
s to cross the ice with
yers under police escort
the entire group could
ia the exit leading to the
g room.

ding to Bloom one of the
fans leaned over and
obscenities at the wo-
the party as they left
en the way to the safer
under the stands and
locked doors.

I taken so much abuse
t and this was just too
said Bloom. "I just
my stick trying to keep
the fans) back and defi:
ad no intention of hitting
man. What the heck, the
re trying to help us."

stitches were taken
e policeman's eye.

e his troubles with police
s Bloom was one of the
ffective Hawk players.

ifth Game
n Television

Catharines Black Hawk
ent Fred Muller said
orning that the fifth
of the Eastern Cana-
unior A hockey finals
day night at Maple
ardens will be carried
annel 11:

ellout is virtually assur-
we felt it was only fair
nable to obtain tick-
use the facilities of
el 11," said Muller.

ut 500 of the 5,300 tick-
signed St. Catharines
have been sold at the
n City Arena box office.
sale here will close at
m. tomorrow.

5th Game – Eastern Canada Finals

Wed., May 12
8 p.m. at
MAPLE LEAF GARDENS

Guy Lafleur

Marcel Dionne

QUEBEC vs. ST. CATHARINES
Tickets On Sale at Garden City Arena

Excellent Choice Of Seats Available. DUE TO DEMAND ANOTHER 2,000 SEATS ARE TO BE MADE AVAILABLE TO ST. CATHARINES FANS!

NO TELEPHONE RESERVATIONS ACCEPTED

BOX and RAIL SEATS and REDS . . . $5.00
BLUES – "SOLD OUT"   GREENS . . $3.00

Garden City Arena Box Office Hours:
Weekdays 10 to 5:30 and 7:30 to 9:30
Sat. and Sun., 10:30 to 5 and 7:30 to 9:30
Get your tickets early . . . the Gardens will be a sellout!

at St. Catharines' two French Canadians, Dionne and Pierre Guite. Dionne, he said, "had every imaginable obscenity directed his way and was also the singled out player by the debris-throwing spectators."

St. Catharines coach Frank Milne, while not condoning the fights, said he had done his best to restrain his players, "but after all the abuse they had taken for two successive nights, I couldn't restrain them any longer."

Thirty-odd years later, Hulme remembers having to back into his net to avoid flying debris. He says fears escalated after the game when it was discovered that a tire on the team bus had been punctured. "Somebody yelled, 'Hey, the bus tire's flat!' and we're all thinking you can't do that to a bus tire with a knife. Somebody must have a gun!" It turned out there was no gun, but that did little to calm the Hawks. Hulme says with a shrug: "We were scared. We were 19 years old." Dionne, on his way out of the rink, spoke briefly to reporters: "It's too bad it happened but you wouldn't believe the amount of tension in a game like that."

BY THE DAY OF GAME 5, A HOME GAME FOR ST. CATHARINES THAT WAS MOVED TO TORONTO'S MAPLE LEAF GARDENS TO ACCOMMODATE THE HUGE DEMAND FOR TICKETS, THE TENSION HAD HARDLY EASED.

In fact, the series seemed on the verge of imploding. The Hawks vowed not to return to the Colisée for Game 6 (assuming a Game 6 was necessary), citing concerns about player safety.

"The kids don't want to go and I don't blame them," said coach Milne. "I don't want to go either and I won't. As far as I'm concerned, under no conditions will we return and be subjected to the abuse from the

HAWKS' LAST STAND: GAME 5 AD IN ST. CATHARINES STANDARD.

fans which we took last weekend. It's a miracle there wasn't a riot."

Hawks' general manager Fred Muller said the team would not return to Quebec without a written guarantee and a $100,000 bond from the CAHA, in effect an insurance policy promising that the Hawks would get adequate police protection. He proposed that Game 6 be played at the Montreal Forum instead, but the plan was nixed by CAHA president Earl Dawson. "There's no way I'm going to let him get me into a position where I'm going to discriminate against people just because they live in the province of Quebec," Dawson told the *Toronto Star*.

Muller claimed he had received a threatening phone call from someone claiming to be a "representative of the FLQ." He added that Marcel Dionne's family in Drummondville had also received threatening calls. "We can't jeopardize the safety of these players, particularly when the parents don't want them to play in Quebec. The parents got together and they are unanimous in their thinking on this point."

None of this posturing was particularly helpful to a 14-year-old hockey fan. The Hawks weren't goons, I knew that, but they had players who certainly weren't afraid to mix it up. I suspected they'd been rougher on their opponents in Quebec than the St. Catharines media had reported. It was hard to deny the evidence from the official scoresheets: defenceman Brian McBratney had been assessed a misconduct and game misconduct for pushing referee Marcel Vaillancourt during Game 3; Hawks forward Brian McKenzie had shoved an official with his stick; Mike Bloom, accidentally or not, had struck a cop in the face.

There are always two sides to every hockey fight, two ways of looking at the root causes of a given donnybrook. But in the Quebec–St. Catharines

26

series, there was a third thing: free-floating paranoia. The players, the fans and the media that covered the series feared the other side in a way that had little to do with hockey and much to do with cultural enmity.

As *Le Soleil*'s Larochelle noted, "The confrontation was tinged with the fanaticism and blind patriotism of a religious crusade. The two clubs, in the midst of this uproar, were sitting on a keg of gunpowder."

In the end, Game 5 was played without incident before 15,343 spectators at Maple Leaf Gardens, an almost sleepy affair. The Hawks won 6-3. Dionne notched two assists. Lafleur scored once.

And so it was that the most vaunted junior rivalry of the era ended not with a bang but a forfeiture. The Hawks refused to return to Quebec and the Remparts were declared the winners. Quebec went on to play the Edmonton Oil Kings for the Memorial Cup, winning a best-of-three series in two straight games at Le Colisée.

Naturally, I felt totally ripped off. Not just because "my team" had lost but because a clash between the game's two prodigies, Lafleur and Dionne, had been interrupted by politics. Quebec claimed (and had some right to claim) that Lafleur had outperformed Dionne, racking up nine points on eight goals and one assist to Dionne's eight points on five goals and three helpers. "He had clearly outshone Dionne," wrote Larochelle. Filion was certain that the best team had won. "I'm confident we would defeat the Hawks even if they did agree to play. Our team was just starting to roll."

Back in St. Catharines, we couldn't help but notice that when the two sides had stuck to hockey, as they had at Maple Leaf Gardens, the Hawks were easy winners. Jim Crerar in the *Toronto Star* wrote that "only superlative play by Quebec goalie Michel Deguise kept Remparts from a complete collapse."

27

The *Star*'s assessment might have been small consolation, but I remember clipping the story for my Hawks scrapbook. In lieu of a Memorial Cup championship, it would have to do.

ON PAPER, THE CAREER NHL STATS OF DIONNE AND LAFLEUR WERE COMPARABLE. THE DIFFERENCE WAS THAT LAFLEUR LED HIS TEAM TO FIVE CHAMPIONSHIPS.

A month later, Guy Lafleur was selected first in the draft by the Montreal Canadiens. Dionne was selected second by the Detroit Red Wings. Both would go on to great careers in the NHL, but Dionne toiled in the relative obscurity of Detroit and Los Angeles, where no Stanley Cup was won during his high-scoring tenure. (Near the end of their playing days, the two old rivals were briefly united as members of the 1988 New York Rangers.)

On paper, their stats were comparable. Dionne rang up 1,771 points (731 goals, 1,040 assists) in 1,348 games during a 19-season career. Lafleur amassed 1,353 points (560 goals, 793 assists) in 1,126 games during a 17-year career.

The difference was that Lafleur led his team to five championships, becoming, in his native Quebec, the natural heir to Rocket Richard and inspiring near religious devotion among his fans. Near the end of his playing days with the Habs, Lafleur spoke about his old rival, Dionne, saying that "maybe he's luckier than me in some ways, to play his whole career without having the pressure ... no Stanley Cups, but maybe saner."

Yes, there was nothing very "sane" about Guy Lafleur's career, which from junior on seemed marked by destiny. Ask anyone from St. Catharines. In the spring of 1971 we learned that he belonged, irrevocably, to the people of Quebec.

Craig MacInnis attended three of the five games in the 1971 junior series between Quebec and St. Catharines.

31

THE SAGA OF

SAD SAM

HOW LAFLEUR

BECAME A HAB

TRADING UP
BY FRANK ORR

THE STORY GOES LIKE THIS: As a young man, Sam Pollock is working in the menswear store owned by his father. One day a grieving widow enters the premises, seeking a dark suit in which to bury her dearly departed husband. Pollock sells her one — with two pairs of pants.

That joke tells you all you need to know about Pollock's flair for getting the best of any deal during his run from 1965 to 1978 as the Montreal Canadiens' general manager and master trader. The yarn was inspired by his larcenous player swaps, which helped boost the Habs to nine Stanley Cup championships in 13 seasons. They won another the year after he left, too, when his imprint was still very much on the roster.

Pollock's most famous trade remains part of NHL folklore, and is recalled for two compelling reasons — to show his smarts as a negotiator, and to underline the folly of a club dealing away its most precious commodity, youth.

In that 1970 deal, Pollock acquired the first-round pick in the 1971 amateur (now entry) draft of the California Golden Seals and, with the selection, picked forward Guy Lafleur. With Lafleur, the Canadiens won five Cups from 1973 to 1979 while the Seals, a team that might have survived with a star of Lafleur's magnitude, departed California to become the Cleveland Barons after five more woeful, money-losing seasons.

33

Sam Pollock started his hockey career in the 1950s as a Montreal-based area scout for the Canadiens and moved into the operation of their junior farm system. Schooled by the master, Frank Selke Sr., who as GM had built the Habs into a hockey dynasty, Pollock learned early the value of strong scouting.

Pollock's career advancement followed a pattern similar to the Canadiens' slow nurturing of their on-ice talent. He was coach and general manager of junior teams, then spent several seasons in minor league professional hockey. When Selke retired, Pollock succeeded him.

He quickly established his expertise in player deals, especially for first-round choices in the entry draft, which became the main source of player talent when the NHL expanded to 12 teams in 1967. If there was a trade that inspired or shocked the hockey world, its author was usually "Sad Sam." That was Pollock's nickname, due to the fact that he often appeared on the verge of tears, which must have elicited sympathy in his adversaries. How else to explain his luck? He'd trade you a rowboat for a battleship. He'd swap you a pork chop for the whole pig.

Pollock made certain that the Canadiens had a large stock of players, many of them minor leaguers, when the NHL doubled its population in 1967. That gave him the opportunity to send packages of fringe NHLers to the new teams in exchange for their future draft choices. Punch Imlach, GM of the Canadiens' chief 1960s rival, the Toronto Maple Leafs, often complained that Leafs ownership had sold off the organization's minor pro clubs, leaving him no excess bodies to match Pollock's deals for draft picks. That created a talent gap between the arch-rivals that was not closed for nearly three decades.

Consider the evidence: In the six entry drafts from 1969 to 1974, the

THE SAGA OF SAD SAM: HOW LAFLEUR BECAME A HAB

Canadiens had 17 first-round and eight second-round selections. In 1972, they picked four times in the first round, five times in 1974.

What's ironic about the Canadiens' exceptional use of the draft is that Pollock was a member of the NHL committee that wrote the rules for both the 1967 expansion and the league's dispersal of amateur talent. He pushed strongly for the inclusion of a clause that would have banned the trading of first-round draft choices, both before the selection was made and for two years afterward. The six expansion team owners objected, arguing that the draft choices were assets of their businesses and that no restrictions should be placed on the way they dispensed their assets.

The deal that consolidated Pollock's reputation was the one that gave Montreal the chance to get Lafleur. Despite winning four Stanley Cups in the five years from 1965 to 1969, the Canadiens were an aging team heading into the 1970s. Their two great French Canadian stars, Jean Beliveau and Henri Richard, were nearing the end of illustrious careers. In the 1969-70 season, it was obvious that the top candidates for first pick in the 1971 draft would be a pair of superb francophones — Lafleur of the Quebec Remparts and Marcel Dionne of the St. Catharines Black Hawks.

The Canadiens–Seals deal was completed on May 22, 1970, and created little stir at the time. The Seals acquired forward Ernie Hicke and the Canadiens' first-round pick in the 1970 draft (centre Chris Oddliefson) in exchange for defenceman Francois Lacombe, some cash and the Seals' first pick in the 1971 draft.

Since the Seals finished with the worst record in the NHL in the 1970-71 season, the Canadiens picked first overall. The words of Garry Young, who had been appointed Seals' GM just before the draft meeting in Montreal, were the death knell for the franchise: "Mr. Campbell [NHL president Clarence], California regretfully defers its first choice to the Stanley Cup champion Montreal Canadiens."

OF COURSE, THE CANADIENS PLUCKED LAFLEUR FROM THE QUEBEC JUNIORS, WHERE HE HAD SCORED 130 GOALS AND 209 POINTS IN 62 GAMES THAT SEASON; 313 GOALS, 538 POINTS IN FOUR SEASONS; 47 GOALS AND 86 POINTS IN 29 PLAYOFF GAMES IN HIS FINAL TWO JUNIOR SEASONS.

Pollock always insisted that the selection was not cut and dried because there was much support among Canadien scouts for Dionne, who had 154 goals and 375 points in 148 games over three seasons for the St. Catharines team.

Another part of the "Flower Fable": when the Los Angeles Kings showed signs of falling below the Seals in futility in the 1970-71 season, Pollock dispatched centre Ralph Backstrom to L.A. for a couple of minor leaguers, giving the Kings a boost in the standings.

It makes for a nifty yarn. The shrewd Pollock, knowing Lafleur with his superstar potential is up for grabs, executes a brilliant forward-thinking trade

to land the opportunity to pick him, then makes a second swap to guarantee his availability.

Years after he departed the Canadiens, Pollock, by then a successful businessman and art collector, strongly denied that was the sequence of events that brought Lafleur to the Habs. He also waved off the "genius" tag many had used to describe his role in the affair.

"In 1969-70, the Seals finished fourth in their division after a strong second-place finish the previous season," Pollock said. "They definitely were a team on their way to good things and many thought they could win the West Division.

The Canadien policy in those days was never to trade away draft choices, but in the deal with the Seals we traded one first-round draft pick for another one. Because the Seals were an improving team, we didn't think there would be much difference between our pick and theirs in 1971. But 1970-71 was a very bad season for the Seals. They had a tough start, and just when they were making a move out of the cellar their best player, defenceman Carol Vadnais, had an ankle injury and missed half the season. The team just collapsed without him.

"There's no way I could have predicted that the Seals would be last in the NHL and we would have their draft pick, No. 1 overall. Sometimes in hockey it's better to be lucky than good."

And what about the Backstrom trade? "Fiction, pure fiction, and stronger words if you want them," Pollock said. "Ralph will verify this. For personal reasons, Ralph wanted to move to a team on the West Coast and we talked about it. He had been a wonderful player for the Canadiens — I had him in Hull-Ottawa on my junior team — and we wanted to grant his wish if possible. He said that he wanted to go to Los Angeles, Oakland or Vancouver and it didn't matter which one. The Kings were the only team to make an offer for him."

And that, according to Sad Sam, is the honest-to-goodness, gospel truth.

Veteran sportswriter Frank Orr was inducted into the Hockey Hall of Fame in 1989.

ROCK
STAR

LIVE AT THE FORUM!
BY MARK LEPAGE

IN THE BEGINNING was the helmet, and the helmet was not good.

Those who remember anything about Guy Lafleur in a helmet — and it is difficult to call to mind, so iconic is the image of that pennant of blond hair — cringe. It was the salad-spinner type, punched with holes and squeezed onto his head as though he were the Great Gazoo. Even with benefit of hindsight, it did not suit him. You do not put sensible shoes on Elvis.

For here in Quebec it was Lafleur's destiny to eventually join the ranks of hockey Elvises (Elvi?) and rock the sport's Graceland, the Montreal Forum. He was arriving as the sports image convulsed along with the culture, when the engines of pop went to work on the players and the game.

NFL football already had Joe Willie Namath and his Broadway boulevardier sensibility; hockey, a late bloomer, had its own young audience raised to worship rock-star style, with new expectations of, and offering new possibilities to its athletes. The fedora era? Gone like Sinatra. No more working stiff, company man, genteel conservative player with the slicked-back hair and the conformist attitude. In Quebec, the 70s were about to explode like a white man's afro. Rebellion was in the air and the audience was primed to embrace a fiery French Canadian sports hero. Lafleur arrived with his small-town Quebec fashion sense — the jacket lapels like B3-bomber wings, the

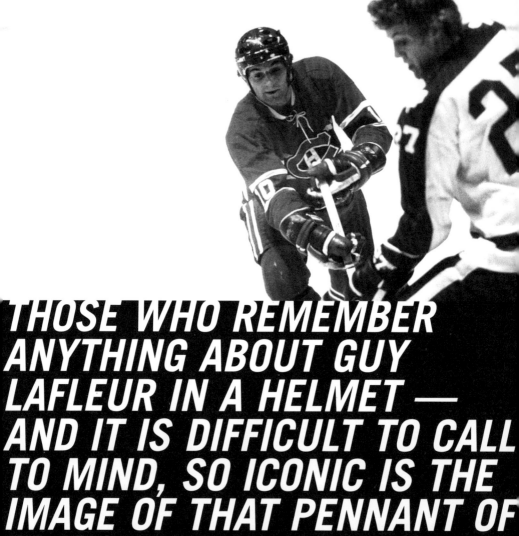

THOSE WHO REMEMBER ANYTHING ABOUT GUY LAFLEUR IN A HELMET — AND IT IS DIFFICULT TO CALL TO MIND, SO ICONIC IS THE IMAGE OF THAT PENNANT OF BLOND HAIR — CRINGE.

sideburns and slightly queasy smile. And he was here to set the night on fire.

Through his first three seasons in the NHL Guy Lafleur flashed prowess, but the man he was replacing (one scorer was always replacing another in Montreal) was the papal Jean Beliveau. Prowess would not be enough. The numbers were reliable, but Lafleur's goal total dropped slightly each year, 29-28-21.

And then it happened. For the second practice of the 1974 training camp Lafleur forgot his helmet in the dressing room, and in Guyville they say his heart grew three sizes that day. Leaving off the helmet removed his anonymity. It put him on stage.

In truth, he was not alone. Before Lafleur arrived, hockey had had a glimpse of the future. Derek Sanderson had already mooked up the joint with a new kind of rock 'n' roll-style flash.

Derek Sanderson: rookie of the year, 1968; two packs a day, 1974. Sanderson (sample quote: "But I like spending money") once legendarily dropped $31,000 cash for a Rolls-Royce because it had started raining. That is Led Zeppelin-grade behaviour, to be sure, and it had required a big-money era and crass tastes to bring it about. Thirteen rehabs later, Sanderson and his booze-broads-and-coke run were done. Anyway, Derek Sanderson lacked a central component of hockey rock stardom: goals. It's one thing to lead the Shane MacGowan lifestyle, but you've got to top the charts, and 202 career goals won't do it.

Among Lafleur's contemporaries, did any have charisma? Bobby Orr was a genius (when they refer to Orr killing a penalty, they mean doing it on his own), but he looked like a graduate of the Andy Griffith show. Now Bobby

SALAD SPINNER DAYS: A HELMETED LAFLEUR
BATTLES LEAFS' DARRYL SITTLER.

FOR HERE IN QUEBEC IT WAS LAFLEUR'S
DESTINY TO EVENTUALLY JOIN THE RANKS OF

HOCKEY ELVISES

(ELVI?) AND ROCK THE SPORTS
GRACELAND, THE MONTREAL FORUM.

Clarke, he had a rocker persona: the bantam thug. Clarke's on-ice demeanour would have fitted in well with a low-rent boogie band like Black Oak Arkansas. Similarly, the other stars of the era — Esposito, Leach, Sittler, Trottier — looked more like lunch-pailers, boiler-roomers, than rock 'n' rollers.

And speaking of pop stars, who can forget Ron Duguay and the New York Rangers "Win A Date With Ron" promotion? The lamentable PR campaign reduced the team's good-looking young star to the level of Donny Osmond, and the games dignity took a serious blow.

Lafleur played for the Habs — no fear of tacky promos there! Sanderson and Clarke had a rock 'n' roll physicality, but were still, in effect, role players, team guys. Guy Lafleur had the talent to be singular — the point on the knife, the lead singer. Still, a great rock star needs motivation, and it must come from within. Mick Jagger had vanity driving him. John Lennon had resentment. Guy Lafleur?

Something had been caged by that salad-spinner helmet, and that something was fear. Most athletes use their talent-born confidence to keep fear at bay: fear of failure, fear of embarrassment, demotion, mortality. They are cosy in that talent. But Lafleur seemed to know that mediocre professionalism and rules would keep him safe, and safe meant being very good, and very good would never be enough. To be great he had to literally lift his head out of the foxhole. To hone his game, he had to thrive on the immediacy of the violence around him. Taking the helmet off made him a target, and it made him faster, and it made him star material. It also revealed him.

While Beliveau seemed almost to glide two inches above the ice, Lafleur was a blood-and-mercury being, with that necessary volatility. His game was not simply numbers. In the era to come, Wayne Gretzky would beat your team

BAND

MC5: FROM LEFT, KEN DRYDEN, MICHEL LAROCQUE, LARRY ROBINSON, LAFLEUR AND BOB GAINEY.

with volume: you can't argue with four goals a game. Lafleur did it as much with the style and timing of his attack. Many players are fast, as befits the sport — a matrix for it — but Guy Lafleur was something like a human speed logo. He moved like a blade, and the most dramatic of his goals had a flourish as much aesthetic as statistical. Teammate Jacques Lemaire approached the game with a tactician's intellect, drawing out play diagrams. Lafleur the improviser had no plan — just a deep intuition of the seeming limitlessness of his gifts,

BY THE MID-70S, A ROCK SHOW IN THE FORUM HAD NOT CLIMAXED UNTIL THE SINGER HAD WORN A LAFLEUR JERSEY ONSTAGE.

acting on the inspiration of the moment, knowing he would score. The Bruins feared it, and with good reason. There are still fans in Boston in denial over the fatal too-many-men power-play goal of the 1979 playoffs. Most, including goalie Gilles Gilbert, have still never even seen the vicious slapshot Lafleur fired to send Game 7 into overtime, setting the table for an eventual Habs victory. The opponent was meant to be awed, to take it personally.

Likewise, Guy did. His persona was as edgy as his game. He could flash a brittle, aggrieved temperament in interviews and had the ego commensurate with his worth. When Marcel Dionne was making three times the salary for scoring empty goals in twilight-zone markets with zero pressure, Lafleur was

ON-ICE, OFF-ICE: ACROSS QUEBEC LAFLEUR
HAD "A CULTURAL IDENTITY TO CARRY."

aggrieved. He threatened to sit out a game in Toronto unless his salary anxieties were addressed. They were. It was the least the Habs could do. Their superstar was winning Stanley Cups and developing the appropriate mythical elements. Tested by team doctors, it was found that he had an unusually strong heart, with a resting rate of 40. This from an athlete who could out-chain-smoke Keith Richards and still play double shifts. Two-packs-a day man, smoking between shifts on the bench, so legend had it in the schoolyards and taverns. In Quebec, where smoking was essentially mandatory, this story alone could make grown men weepy. Here was the hero-artist in every workingman's imagining of himself, and the hero had the same liver-and-lung-punishing tastes.

The Quebecois hockey fan has an exaggerated connection to his team and its players. In no other hockey culture does the sport mix into the volatile bloodstream of politics, language and sense of self. Here in the land of perpetual insecurity, the homegrown superstar is aspiration made flesh, a vent where the steam of doubt escapes and, hitting the air, becomes pride. It is not enough to win: a French Canadian player has a cultural identity to carry.

By the time Québécois clown prince rockeur Robert Charlebois toasted him from the stage of the Big O during a concert, Lafleur meant everything. By the mid-70s, a rock show in the Forum had not climaxed until the singer had worn a Lafleur jersey onstage. (This made for much hilarity as an Ozzy Osbourne or Rodger Hodgson or some other stoned Brit with no clue about a "Lafloor" took the mike and led the collective ovation. And then, "Fools Overture"!)

Less hilarious was a hush-hush kidnap plot involving bank robbers who targeted Lafleur in 1976 during the Habs playoff run. Fortunately, the bad guys were apprehended before Lafleur came to any harm. A true celebrity now, he owned guns for protection. Meanwhile, and in keeping with the times, he was ripening his own appetite for some of the lifestyle habits suitable to a star. There were endorsements for sticks, skates, soft drinks, yogurt. Lafleur had apparently felt uncomfortable in Montreal when he first arrived. He was never going to be a Derek Sanderson, much less a Jagger, but now he came to like the big city and he came to like the discos.

Thursdays, Gatsbys, Privé, Saga, 1234 ... Lafleur became known in some circles as the King of Crescent Street, Montreal's glitz-tacky party strip. Canadiens management had already forced him to get rid of a Ferrari; now GM Irving Grundman wanted him to lose a Harley-Davidson.

"Play every game as if it is your last one," Lafleur would say when he retired for the second time, from the Quebec Nordiques. He nearly lived down to that in March 1981, when Montrealers awoke to find Guy Lafleur on the front page instead of in the sports section. After a night on the town and the begging of his friends for the keys to his Cadillac, Lafleur fell asleep while his beast of a car was tanking westbound along Highway 20. The car left the roadway and took out several yards of security fencing, ripping through it with such dumb force that the windshield was speared by a metal pole. Although Lafleur survived, a piece of his right earlobe was sheared off — the idiot tax. In the photos of the aftermath, the pole runs up the length of the hood and right through the windshield and the steering wheel. Had he not been asleep, he would have been decapitated. Not even a helmet would have saved him. Lafleur, who must surely have been above the legal limit for impairment, was never charged and his earlobe was repaired.

HAB LEGENDS: LAFLEUR AND GOALIE KEN DRYDEN.

MICK JAGGER HAD VANITY DRIVING HIM. JOHN LENNON HAD RESENTMENT. GUY LAFLEUR?

The Habs were in decline by the early 1980s. We will never know if something in his motivation had been diluted, cured or paid in full, or if it was the Habs new defensive system (under a succession of coaches, including Jacques Lemaire), but Lafleur was over as a chart-topper. It was time for Wayne's World.

By any measure, Lafleur was the game's shining icon of the mid to late 1970s. The Canadiens won when he was great, when he was the zooming spirit in the perfect machine, and they were dunned to mediocrity when he faltered. After 13 years as a Hab, he hung up his skates in November of '84. Over the next 20 years, his former team, lacking magic, would manage to win only two Cups.

Then Lafleur did something perfectly Lafleur. He came out of retirement

53

HAB LEGENDS: LAFLEUR AND GOALIE KEN DRYDEN.

THE CANADIENS WON WHEN HE WAS GREAT, WHEN HE WAS THE ZOOMING SPIRIT IN THE PERFECT MACHINE, AND THEY WERE DUNNED TO MEDIOCRITY WHEN HE FALTERED.

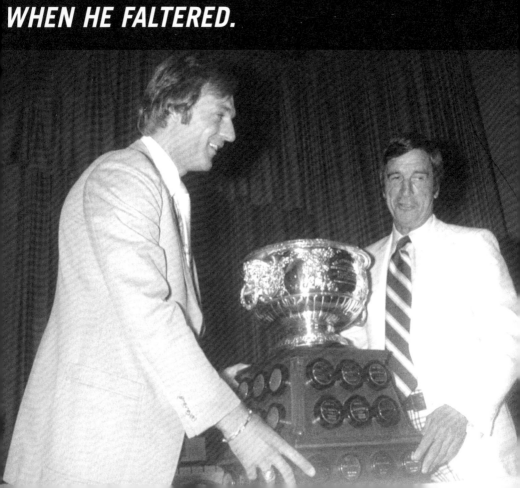

and joined the New York Rangers for the 1988-89 season. He went on tour again. Yet unlike those rock stars who hang around and come back and hit the road without their bassist or their upper octave or their hairline, Guy's comeback felt justified, and instructive. It was a rare opportunity to confront mortality in sport, and to catch flashes of a talent that used to be fluid and unified: a feint, a deke, a display of stickhandling as stylish and precise as a fencing attack. Perhaps it was the first time we really believed he could do all that.

There is one final parallel with rock: I find the players and the game today match the music at its most masculine edge, which is hard rock: bigger, angrier, more testosterone-fuelled, and less creative. Lafleur was using the same repertoire as every other player — slapshot, wrist shot, backhand, deke and feint, shake-and-bake — but at his best his play was creative and not careerist. It was music to your eyes.

Mark Lepage is a former rock critic for the Montreal Gazette. *He writes on pop culture from New York.*

"I'D LIKE TO THANK MY FANS ...": LAFLEUR ACCEPTS THE ART ROSS TROPHY FOR WINNING THE NHL SCORING TITLE FROM PREVIOUS RECIPIENT TED LINDSAY.

A LATE-BLOOMING FLOWER

BY FRANK ORR

EACH ERA HAS ONE, that certain someone whose presence is so all-consuming that his name becomes synonymous with the game.

Cyclone Taylor was the first — the explosive "rover" who rocked the hockey world during the first two decades of the 20th century. Howie Morenz assumed the role in the 1920s as the spectacular star of the Montreal Canadiens and an important attraction in the National Hockey League's growth in the U.S. Eddie Shore, the surly but highly skilled rearguard of the Boston Bruins, boosted the game through the 1930s.

Opposing titans Maurice Richard of the Canadiens and Gordie Howe of the Detroit Red Wings created big post-World War II interest in pro hockey, setting off debates that rage to this day over who was better.

In the 1960s, "the Golden Jet," Bobby Hull of the Chicago Black Hawks, raised the game's profile in the U.S. with his rugged charm and awesome scoring feats, which helped trigger league expansion in 1967. Off the ice, his move to the World Hockey Association (WHA) in 1972 was the catalyst for huge increases in hockey salaries.

Bobby Orr, maybe the finest pure talent hockey has seen, forever altered the complexion of the game with his unprecedented offensive exploits during the late 1960s and early 1970s. When Orr's career was shortened by injuries,

57

Wayne Gretzky took over as the NHL's main man, leading the Edmonton Oilers, a team that had risen from the ashes of the old WHA, to dominance in the 1980s. With his trade to Los Angeles in 1988, Gretzky not only added unprecedented cachet to the game in trendy lotus land, but inspired deeper expansion into the southern U.S. Mario Lemieux of the Pittsburgh Penguins

WHEN ORR'S CAREER WAS SHORTENED BY INJURIES, *WAYNE GRETZKY TOOK OVER AS THE NHL'S MAIN MAN.*

was Gretzky's equal in talent and offensive production but injuries and illness plagued him during what should have been his peak playing years.

To many, however, this timeline is not quite complete. It's easy to forget, but for six marvellous seasons between Orr's painful leave-taking and the rise of "the Great One" no one dominated hockey like Guy Lafleur. From 1974 to 1980, Lafleur raised the level of his game to breathtaking heights.

BOOKENDS: BOBBY ORR DEFINED THE GAME BEFORE LAFLEUR; AFTERWARD, IT WAS GRETZKY'S TURN.

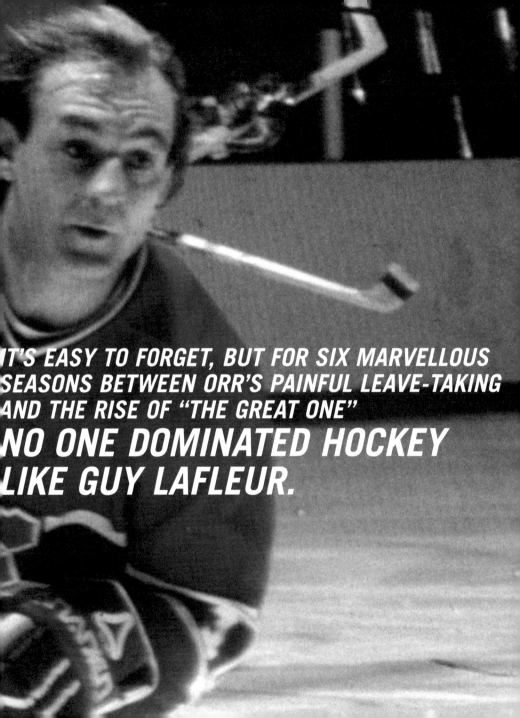

IT'S EASY TO FORGET, BUT FOR SIX MARVELLOUS SEASONS BETWEEN ORR'S PAINFUL LEAVE-TAKING AND THE RISE OF "THE GREAT ONE" NO ONE DOMINATED HOCKEY LIKE GUY LAFLEUR.

In the 462 games he played during those years, he scored 327 goals and 439 assists for 766 points, earned six first-team all-star selections, three scoring titles, six consecutive 50-goal seasons, twice was awarded the Hart Trophy as most valuable player and three times collected the Pearson Trophy as the league's outstanding player as chosen by his peers, the members of the NHL Players' Association.

In the pressure of the Stanley Cup playoffs, Lafleur's star shone even brighter. After making a modest contribution to the Habs' Stanley Cup victory in his second season, 1972-73, he led the team to four consecutive crowns from 1976 to 1979 with 36 goals and 41 assists for 87 points in 68 playoff games. At his best in crunch situations, Lafleur counted 11 game-winning scores in that stretch. He won the Conn Smythe Trophy as playoff MVP in 1977.

If there is an argument against Lafleur's inclusion in hockey's list of super-luminaries, it is the three seasons that preceded and the eight that followed his six-season reign. It's not that he wasn't good then. It's just that no one, not even Lafleur himself, could match what he did in his glory years. In his half dozen best seasons, in which he played 41 percent of his 1,126 games, he produced 58 percent of his career goals and 56 percent of his total points.

Lafleur was among the most widely publicized junior stars ever when he racked up 313 goals and 538 points in four terms with the Quebec Remparts, including 103 and 130 goals in his final two seasons. By the standards expected of him, the Flower was slow to bloom in Montreal. His numbers (29 goals as a rookie, a 78-97-175 point total in his first three seasons) were excellent in comparison to the early stats of many top-level stars, but it earned him an initial "big disappointment" tag in Montreal.

In the seasons after his six wonder years (five-plus with the Canadiens, then one with the New York Rangers and two with the Quebec Nordiques in a comeback at age 37 after a three-year retirement), Lafleur achieved respectable offensive numbers. But his greatness showed only in flashes.

At his best, he was the complete package. At six feet and 180 pounds, he didn't have the size to play a truly physical game but he never shied away from contact. His teammate, goalie Ken Dryden, wrote an exceptional book, The Game, in which he summarized perfectly the Lafleur approach: "[S]ince his early disappointing seasons, Lafleur has learned what Muhammad Ali learned before him — that if you're quick enough, you can play a hitting game and rarely get hit. It was a crucial discovery. Confidence, he called it, comfort knowing he could play with dazzling abandon, using all his special skills, undistracted, undeterred by intimidation, protected by nothing but his legs."

Lafleur's acceleration to top speed consumed less time and a lower number of strides than that of any other player of his era. "If Flower was a drag racer, he would hold all the speed records," said Steve Shutt, Lafleur's left-wing linemate in the Canadiens' glory years. "His acceleration was scary. I never saw a better 'first step' in hockey, that ability to just 'ping' off the mark or to take his speed up a few notches instantaneously."

While his quickness and speed allowed him to play a "hit-and-run" game and avoid heavy checks, Lafleur absorbed extreme punishment from opponents' sticks — hooks, slashes and cross-checks that would have caused lesser players to retaliate in kind. Lafleur never seemed even to flinch or grimace, so determined was he to play on.

"Guy's 'retaliation' would not be to go whack the back of the guy who had whacked him," said Canadiens' coach Scotty Bowman. "Instead, he would get even by gritting his teeth, digging in a little harder, and embarrassing his opponent with a big offensive move."

Quickness and skating agility were the foundations of Lafleur's skill set. He had superb hands for handling and passing the puck and especially for shooting it. He was a gifted scorer, with access to a full repertoire of dekes and feints on scoring chances close to the net. More important, he had an exceptional shot from almost anywhere on the ice — a short-swing "snapper" from the high slot, say, or that blistering slapshot off the wing.

His skating agility and puck control allowed him to play havoc with defences, giving his linemates Shutt and, for most of the glory years, centre Jacques Lemaire, the extra second or two they needed to free themselves for a pass.

Away from the puck, Lafleur was a master at locating open ice. "When the Canadiens rushed our zone, I always was happier to see the Flower with the puck than someone else," said Brad Park, a Hall Of Fame defenceman for the Boston Bruins. "If he had it, then you had a chance to defend against him, to rush him and force a pass or try to skate him out of the play. But if another guy brought it into our zone, that meant Lafleur could float around, going all over the place to get clear for a pass and pulling our defensive alignment all out of kilter. He was so quick that he could get away from even the tightest coverage, needing only to get a pass and unload that shot."

That Lafleur could not maintain his high standards during his later years came as no surprise to those who knew him well.

"Flower's intensity about the game was at such a high level that it had to take a toll on him," said Shutt, who was Lafleur's roommate and close friend for much of their time with the Canadiens. "There never was another player

"HIS ACCELERATION WAS SCARY. I NEVER SAW A BETTER 'FIRST STEP' IN HOCKEY, THAT ABILITY TO JUST 'PING' OFF THE MARK OR TO TAKE HIS SPEED UP A FEW NOTCHES INSTANTANEOUSLY."

that I've heard of like him that way. Cripes, on game days he often would be to the dressing room by two in the afternoon for an eight o'clock game. I can remember going early for injury treatment and at three o'clock Flower was dressed for the game with his skates done up tight. A half hour later he would be down to his underwear, getting dressed and undressed two or three times."

Old habits die hard. When Canadiens and Oilers alumni played in the November 2003 Heritage Classic old-timers' game on an outdoor rink at Commonwealth Stadium in Edmonton, Lafleur was in his hockey gear four hours before the opening faceoff.

The great Bobby Orr was nearing the end of his extraordinary but far too brief NHL career when he staged his last hockey hurrah as a member of Team Canada in the first Canada Cup in 1976. Orr's teammate, making his international debut, was Lafleur.

"For me to play on my beat-up old wheels, I had to spend almost the whole month of the tournament with my knees in ice," Orr recalled years later. "On game days, especially, I would be encased in ice for hours at the rink. But I wasn't alone. Lafleur would be there early in the afternoon, walking the corridors, drinking one Coke after another and chain-smoking cigarettes. He would put his equipment and uniform, skates included, on and take it off several times. He would be so wound up that he didn't say much."

Mid-career, Lafleur spoke candidly about his priorities. "I really love my family, especially my wife and son," he said. "But my career, my hockey, comes first in my life. Once in a while, the fans come second and my family is third. It changes all the time."

Many close to the Canadiens in that era claim that the seemingly early decline in Lafleur's play was no surprise. His heavy smoking had to take a toll on his stamina and his penchant for living life to the fullest was legendary.

"To be honest about it, the Flower did not take the greatest care of himself in his first 10 years or so in the NHL," said one teammate from the Habs' glory days. "He lived in the fast lane, and not just in the fast cars he drove. The way he played the game was the way he lived his life — flat out every second. Add to that how many high-pressure games he was in, competition that was that way because the team was so great and the fans' expectations were so high, and the incredible standards Guy set for himself, the effort he had to produce to reach and stay at that level, and it's little wonder he couldn't stay on that plateau forever."

To those privileged enough to watch Lafleur during those six wonderful seasons, there was no doubt about it — he was as good as anyone who ever played the game.

Former NHL beat writer Frank Orr was in the press box for many of Lafleur's greatest games.

THE
BROAD STREET
BULLIES
MEET THEIR MATCH

FLOWER FOILS THE FLYERS
BY DOUG HEROD

I HATED THE PHILADELPHIA FLYERS of the mid-1970s. Bunch of rotten no-goodniks! They were brash, belligerent and barbaric. Worse, for those worried about the future of hockey, they were highly successful: nothing breeds imitation in sports like success. Where oh where were the Montreal Canadiens to deliver us from evil? The Habs were the most successful franchise in hockey history, yet one whose elegance and style were somewhat out of fashion in the rough-and-tumble 1970s.

Yeah, I know. The Canadiens weren't exactly chopped liver in the early part of the decade, having won the Cup in 1971 and 1973. And they had drafted Quebec junior legend Guy Lafleur, one of the most celebrated prospects since Bobby Orr. But as Lafleur stumbled out of the gate, it seemed the famed *bleu, blanc et rouge* no longer had cachet. Successful to varying degrees, yes, but no longer the NHL's "it" team. That label had been taken by the Bruins and, latterly, the Flyers.

Head-manning the puck was out, an elbow to the chops was in. The dashing winger was dead, long live the Cro-Magnon basher! Welcome to the new National Hockey League, as exemplified by the Broad Street Bullies of Philadelphia. Winners of two consecutive Stanley Cups, Philadelphia was intent on mugging its way to a "three-peat" in 1976, a journey that reached its nadir that

69

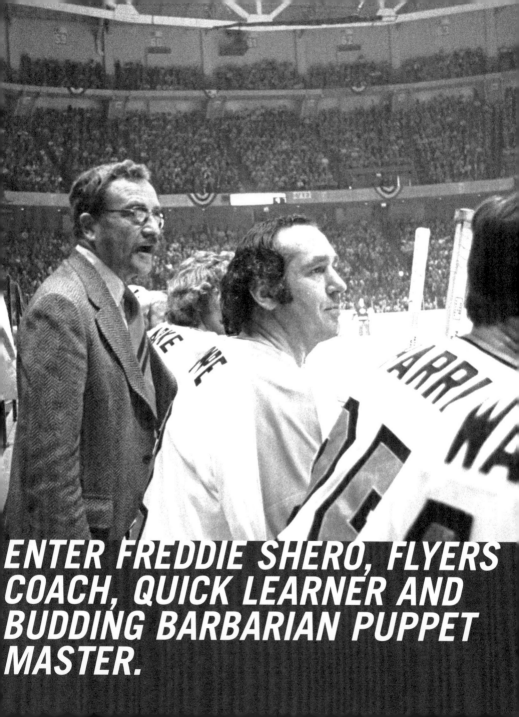

ENTER FREDDIE SHERO, FLYERS COACH, QUICK LEARNER AND BUDDING BARBARIAN PUPPET MASTER.

spring in a violence-filled quarter-final against the Toronto Maple Leafs.

Let's roll some archival film footage in our minds. There's beetle-browed Mel Bridgman smashing his knuckles against the bloodied face of unwilling combatant Borje Salming as the star Leaf defenceman lies on the ice. Following the game, Bridgman and teammates Joe Watson and Don Saleski faced criminal charges from Toronto police for their violent behaviour. No matter. Flyers punched out a series win in seven. Their rabid supporters cheered. The team marched on to the finals and the Broad Street Bullies continued to stand for all that was bad, ugly and goonish about the game of hockey.

Not that I didn't enjoy watching the odd tussle, donnybrook or pier-sixer over the years. But when I look back, wearing the rose-tinted glasses of middle age, I recall that most hockey brawls in pre-Flyer times had a certain spontaneity to them. Or, if the punch-ups were premeditated, at least the combatants weren't one-dimensional thugs. The Bobby Orr-era Bruins were no angels (hence their "Big Bad Bruins" tag), but Wayne Cashman, Derek Sanderson, Johnny McKenzie and Don Awrey weren't just bruisers for hire, either. These guys played key and full-time roles in the team's considerable success. And the violence of the Bruins was always a sideshow to the offensive brilliance of Orr, Esposito, Johnny Bucyk and company. Mind you, from the vantage point of my living room the Bruins' willingness to fight, particularly in the confined space of the Boston Garden, seemed to have an intimidating effect on many opponents. Evidently, I wasn't the only one who noticed. Enter Freddie Shero, Flyers coach, quick learner and budding barbarian puppet master.

Most observers looking at the Flyers lineup in the early 1970s wouldn't have pegged the team as a future Stanley Cup winner. Philly had superb goaltending,

FOG OF WAR: FLYERS COACH FRED SHERO.

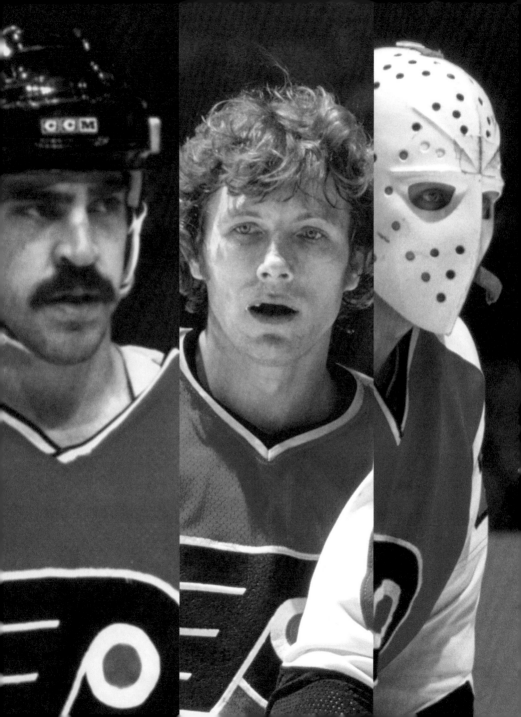

HOUSE OF HORRORS?: FROM LEFT,
MEL BRIDGMAN, BOBBY CLARKE, BERNIE PARENT,
DAVE SCHULTZ, BILL BARBER AND BOB KELLY.

a solid defence corps, the talented and hard-working (if cretinous) Bobby Clarke, and several snipers. But they lacked pedigree and flash. The latter qualities were irrelevant in the grand scheme of "Freddie the Fog."

Shero drilled into his players, with Clarke serving as a terrific role model, an unsurpassed tenacity for checking — along the boards, in front of the net, in the corners. Indeed, wherever the puck was, a Flyer would soon be arriving. Shero simplified, if that was possible, Conn Smythe's old dictum "If you can't beat 'em in the alley, you can't beat 'em on the ice" to "If you can beat 'em up on the ice, you can beat 'em on the ice." He loaded his squad with thugs like Moose Dupont, Dave Schultz, Bob Kelly and Don Saleski.

Unfortunately, it worked. Hockey was going to hell in a handcart led by the aforementioned Four Knuckleheads of the Apocalypse. Then again, maybe not. The cavalry, in the form of the Montreal Canadiens, was positioning itself for a possible rescue. The perception of hockey as roller derby on ice began to change, however slightly, as we entered the second half of the decade with the re-emergence of the Habs as a dominant force and the blossoming of their star right-winger, Guy Lafleur.

Lafleur had entered the league to great fanfare in the fall of 1971 following his astonishing junior hockey career, during which he had scored a zillion points and led his Quebec Remparts to Canada's top junior hockey crown. He didn't exactly stink up the joint in his first three years as a Hab, but nor did he live up to his advanced billing as the second coming of Rocket Richard. He took a quantum leap forward in his fourth season, finishing fourth in league scoring. The next year was even better as he won his first of three straight scoring titles. And he did it with a flair that seemed to inspire the rest of the squad, bringing to mind the "Flying Frenchmen" of years past. The

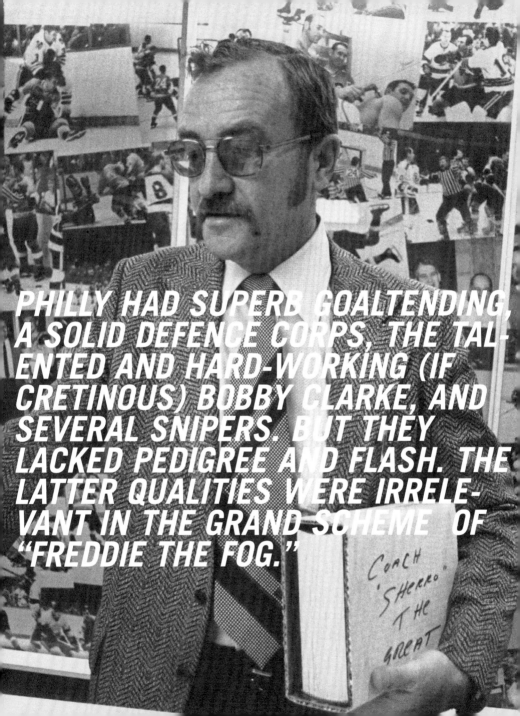

PHILLY HAD SUPERB GOALTENDING, A SOLID DEFENCE CORPS, THE TALENTED AND HARD-WORKING (IF CRETINOUS) BOBBY CLARKE, AND SEVERAL SNIPERS. BUT THEY LACKED PEDIGREE AND FLASH. THE LATTER QUALITIES WERE IRRELEVANT IN THE GRAND SCHEME OF "FREDDIE THE FOG."

COACH "SHERRO" THE GREAT

Canadiens finished atop the NHL standings in the 1975-76 regular season, and did it playing a hard-checking but wonderfully clean style of hockey — in contrast to their main competition, the Flyers.

Nowhere was this contrast sharper than during a couple of exhibition games that year with Moscow's Central Red Army squad, whose members included several players from the epic 1972 Summit Series. The Red Army played Montreal on New Year's Eve in a game for the ages. It was a free-flowing, fast-paced, cleanly played affair that had an appreciative Forum crowd on its feet for most of its 60 minutes. It ended in a 3-3 tie and, afterward, one sensed that players from both teams appreciated and respected each others' skill and style. Two weeks later, the Soviets met the Flyers before a jingoistic mob in Philadelphia. The Flyers played their usual brutal, take-no-prisoners style and cowed the Red Army into subservience. I refuse to believe I was the only North American who found the experience painful to watch.

Montreal cruised through the early rounds of the playoffs that year; Philadelphia had it tougher. No matter. The stage was set for a classic final, pitting the Flyers, proud accumulators of a record 1,980 penalty minutes, against the Canadiens, who had served a mere 977 minutes in the box. Would hockey supremacy be symbolized by Dave "the Hammer" Schultz or Guy "the Flower" Lafleur?

Yee-haw, the Canadiens won! In four straight! Hockey was saved! The speed and energy of the Habs forwards haunted the Flyers defence throughout the series, a bedevilling best illustrated by Lafleur stealing the puck from Tom Bladon in the second game and then potting the unassisted winning goal.

In a delicious comment on the limitations of thuggery, Toronto Star columnist Jim Proudfoot noted that "in an act of mercy," fist-ready but skill-challenged

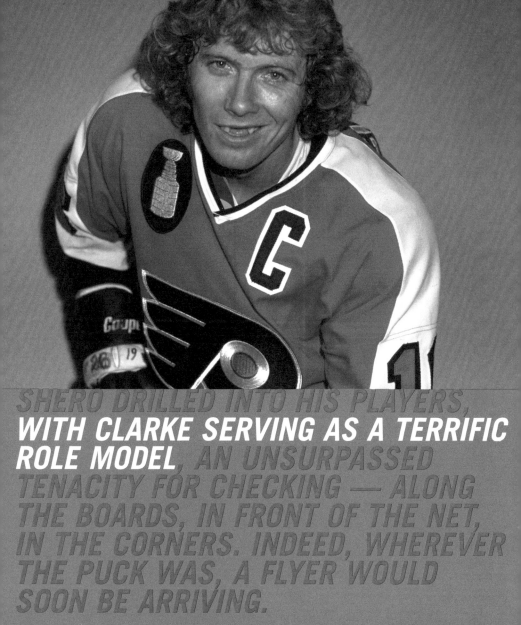

SHERO DRILLED INTO HIS PLAYERS,
**WITH CLARKE SERVING AS A TERRIFIC
ROLE MODEL,** AN UNSURPASSED
TENACITY FOR CHECKING — ALONG
THE BOARDS, IN FRONT OF THE NET,
IN THE CORNERS. INDEED, WHEREVER
THE PUCK WAS, A FLYER WOULD
SOON BE ARRIVING.

defenceman Jack McIlhargey had been removed from the Flyers lineup early in the Cup final. "He had been doing a splendid imitation of a revolving door."

But let's be fair. While Montreal was a relatively low-penalty team, it wasn't composed of figure skaters. The players were big, strong and tough-minded. Yes, Lafleur played well, if somewhat inconspicuously in the final — he led the team in scoring with seven points, including a goal and two assists in the fourth game — but he wasn't the only reason the Habs won. Much chatter focused on their big and mobile defence of Larry Robinson, Guy Lapointe and Serge Savard as well as Montreal's willingness to bump and check with Philly. No team has won a Stanley Cup since 1975 employing the out-and-out hooliganism of the Flyers. By the same token, no team has won a championship since then without toughness of mind and body. And that includes the great Montreal squads of the late 1970s, which, led by Lafleur's virtuoso performances, defeated some very aggressive and hard-checking teams in the playoffs.

His tying goal late in the third period of Game 7 in the 1979 series against Boston, a series won by the Habs in overtime, is one of those vignettes for the ages — a give-and-go with centre Jacques Lemaire, then the howitzer-like slapshot from the streaking Lafleur. It's seared into the consciousness of every hockey fan.

You could make the case that Lafleur put an end to coach Don Cherry's career in Boston, which didn't prevent "Grapes" from paying his nemesis a grudging compliment: "If it wasn't for that guy, I'd have a couple of Stanley Cup rings to wear."

Lafleur's artistry, of course, didn't put a stop to fighting around the league. But at least the premeditated, mass-mayhem approach of the Flyers became a relic of the Slapshot '70s. Now, more often, it's a case of a team keeping a cruise missile at the end of its bench to combat the other team's ICBM. Every once in a while they emerge from their silos, go out on the ice, destroy each other and then the game continues.

Would team brawling be more pervasive in today's NHL if the Flyers had knocked off the Canadiens in 1976? Who knows? But I'm glad Guy Lafleur was around at a very unsettling time in hockey history to prove might doesn't necessarily make right.

Three cheers for Flower Power!

Hockey purist Doug Herod is a columnist for the St. Catharines Standard.

GUY'S GREATEST GAME

BY FRANK ORR

BEFORE THE SERIES OPENED, Boston coach Don Cherry predicted good things for his Bruins "if we can just control that damned Lafleur." Cherry, having been burned so often in the past, knew it wouldn't be easy.

When a National Hockey League player achieves the greatness of a Guy Lafleur, his myth is built on those extraordinary moments that not only influence the outcome of a major contest but define the memories of an entire generation of fans.

It happened countless times for Lafleur, his list of Herculean efforts seemingly endless. But to many fans his most dramatic performance came in the seventh game of the 1979 Stanley Cup playoff semifinal series against the Boston Bruins. As a Montreal columnist in the Montreal Forum press box that May evening noted: "The Canadiens wanted to lose that game but Lafleur wouldn't let them."

The Bruins were the Canadiens' strongest rivals during the Montreal club's four consecutive Cup championships from 1976 to 1979. The teams met in the 1977 and 1978 final and the semifinal in 1979. The Bruins had improved each year. After a Canadiens sweep in 1977, Boston pushed hard in a grinding six-game loss in 1978 and, by the following spring, were confident that their time had come.

Cherry famously described his charges as "a lunch-bucket team of workers," a hard-labouring club with good skills that used effort and muscle to compete with the quicker, more talented Habs. Before the series opened, he issued his famous quote about keeping a lid on "that damned Lafleur."

The series was a roller-coaster ride of excellent, high-speed, ultra-com-

BEFORE THE SERIES OPENED, BOSTON COACH DON CHERRY PREDICTED GOOD THINGS FOR HIS BRUINS

"IF WE CAN JUST CONTROL THAT DAMNED LAFLEUR."

petitive games, the tension boosted by the verbal exchanges of the coaches, Cherry and Scotty Bowman of the Canadiens. The flashily dressed Cherry, who would become a fixture on *Hockey Night in Canada* telecasts a few years later, even poked fun at the conservative attire of his rival.

The Canadiens won the first two games of the series in Montreal, 4-2 and 5-2, but the Bruins fought back in two tough games at the Boston Garden, winning 3-2 on a late goal by defenceman Brad Park, then 4-3 on an overtime goal by centre Jean Ratelle to even the series. The Canadiens dominated the fifth game at home, 5-1, but the Bruins rebounded with a 5-2 win to send the series to a one-game finale.

The atmosphere was highly charged for the decisive game at the Montreal Forum, a building that had been the scene of countless critical

COACH IS CORNERED: BRUINS' DON CHERRY,
STYMIED TIME AND AGAIN BY LAFLEUR.

contests during the Canadiens' lengthy history. Many times, one of the team's great stars would produce an extraordinary feat — a big goal, an uncanny defensive move, a brilliant save — to tilt the outcome in the Habs' favour. But few of those superb efforts could match the performance of Lafleur against the Bruins that night. Any time the picture went black for the home side, the Flower turned on a light.

WHILE BOSTON EXTENDED MONTREAL TO THE ABSOLUTE LIMIT WITH A SOLID TEAM EFFORT, **THE WORK OF BRUINS GOALIE GILLES GILBERT WAS PIVOTAL.**

Gilbert had replaced veteran Gerry Cheevers early in the series and excelled. At times, the seventh game seemed to be a two-man battle, Lafleur vs. Gilbert. The Canadiens threw 52 shots at Gilbert while the Bruins managed only 32 on Ken Dryden.

This was in the era before players' ice time was recorded by the NHL, but a Hab spokesman later said Lafleur clocked 46 minutes of the 69-minute, 33-second game. He was on the ice for at least six minutes of the 9:33 overtime, meaning that he played the equivalent of two complete periods during the regulation contest.

"I don't remember playing more minutes in a game in my career than that one against the Bruins," Lafleur said years later. "But what difference did it make? We had to do everything possible to beat a team that just wouldn't give up. We had several players who seemed to be on the ice all night. I wasn't the only one who worked a little overtime."

Rick Middleton gave the Bruins the first-period lead, with Jacques Lemaire tying the score for the Canadiens. In the second, the Bs appeared to have the game under control, taking a 3-1 lead on two goals by Wayne Cashman.

FLOWER FODDER: BOSTON GOALIE GILLES GILBERT HAD HIS HANDS FULL WITH HABS' NO. 10.

TRAFFIC JAM: LAFLEUR FLOATS FREE AS HABS ATTACK THE BOSTON NET.

"We had some big chances by uncovered players with clear shots in the first 40 minutes," Bowman said. "But it looked like some absolutely great goaltending was going to beat us."

But Lafleur would have no part of it. Playing almost nonstop in the third period, the Flower mounted a mesmerizing comeback. In the first sequence, he sped down the boards into the Bruin zone and, while being forced behind the net by a Boston checker, one-handed a pass to Mark Napier for a quick scoring shot at 6:16.

Two minutes later on a power play, Lafleur's superb puck control allowed him to get clear enough to feed a pass to defenceman Guy Lapointe for a game-tying 50-foot slapper.

The Canadiens, with Lafleur leading the charge, continued to press, forcing Gilbert to make a succession of tough stops. But when Lapointe was carried off on a stretcher with a knee injury, the life seemed to go out of the home team. The Bruins scored what appeared to be the winning goal at 16:01 of the third when Middleton dipped out from the side of the net and buried it.

Sensing defeat, the Forum crowd went silent — until one of the NHL's milestone historical moments, a penalty to the Bruins at 17:26 for too many men on the ice. Lafleur played a large role in the call. Boston's manpower violation was the result of a hurry-up change as the Bruins tried to keep tenacious winger Don Marcotte out on the ice against the Flower. Cherry took the blame for the mix-up.

"It was my fault, nobody else's," Cherry said. "Get caught with too many men at that stage and it's the coach's fault. Two of our guys heard me yell and away they went. If I hadn't grabbed a couple more we would have had eight or nine, not seven, on the ice."

THIS WAS IN THE ERA BEFORE PLAYERS' ICE TIME WAS RECORDED BY THE NHL, BUT A HAB SPOKESMAN LATER SAID LAFLEUR CLOCKED 46 MINUTES OF THE 69-MINUTE, 33-SECOND GAME.

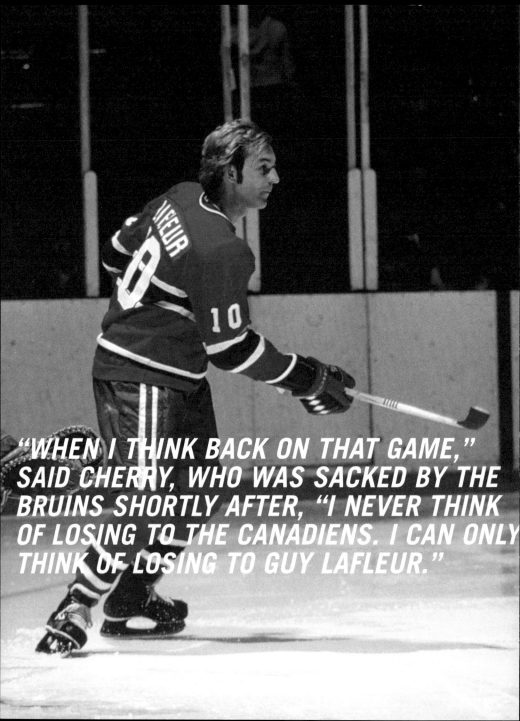

"WHEN I THINK BACK ON THAT GAME," SAID CHERRY, WHO WAS SACKED BY THE BRUINS SHORTLY AFTER, "I NEVER THINK OF LOSING TO THE CANADIENS. I CAN ONLY THINK OF LOSING TO GUY LAFLEUR."

Lafleur both started and finished the play for the goal that rescued the game for the Habs. From just outside the Canadiens' zone, he relayed the puck to centre Jacques Lemaire near the Bruins' blue line. Lemaire moved along the boards into Bruins territory, then shoved the puck slowly toward the middle of the ice. Lafleur arrived at full speed with his stick cocked. Before Gilbert could move out to cut down the angle, the puck was past him and into the far side.

"Lafleur unloaded the hardest shot I ever saw in a lifetime in hockey," Cherry said. "There was no way anyone could have stopped it."

Lafleur had three chances to end the game in overtime but, on one of the Flower's few visits to the bench, winger Yvon Lambert did the job, racing to the net to shove Mario Tremblay's pass between Gilbert's skates to give the Canadiens the win.

"When I think back on that game," said Cherry, who was sacked by the Bruins shortly after, "I never think of losing to the Canadiens. I can only think of losing to Guy Lafleur."

Veteran hockey journalist Frank Orr covered the 1979 Montreal–Boston series for the *Toronto Star*.

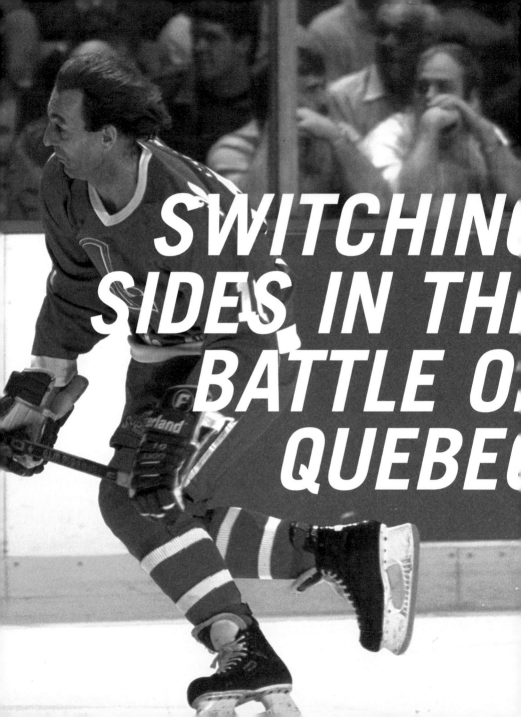

SWITCHING
SIDES IN THE
BATTLE OF
QUEBEC

HERO'S HOMECOMING
BY CRAIG MacINNIS

POETICALLY, GUY LAFLEUR'S CAREER came full circle when he inked a deal with the Quebec Nordiques in the summer of 1989, 18 years after graduating from the city's junior Remparts.

The news conference to announce his signing was emotion-charged as a crowd of 150 in the ritzy Château Bonne Entente began clapping and chanting "Guy! Guy! Guy!" As the *Montreal Gazette*'s Pat Hickey noted: "It was like a family homecoming, a point that was emphasized by the banner that hung behind Lafleur. It contained the Quebec Remparts logo and the number 4 and it was first unfurled when the junior team retired his number."

"I picked Quebec because I know the city and I know my family can be comfortable here," Lafleur said.

Hockey fan Jacques Grosset, 30, of Granby, told the *Gazette* that he would have to change allegiances. "We usually root for the Canadiens but I think we'll follow Lafleur."

Lafleur would prove to be just as popular with his new teammates. Before the all-star break that first season with the Nords, he was invited to captain the Wales Conference team but declined. He insisted that Joe Sakic, Quebec's leading scorer, be on the team instead.

"It will be great for him to go," the 38-year-old Lafleur said of his

93

FULL CIRCLE: LAFLEUR AS A QUEBEC NORDIQUE —
IN THE CITY WHERE IT ALL STARTED.

NOWHERE WAS LAFLEUR MORE INCREDIBLE TO WATCH THAN IN HIS RETURN TO THE MONTREAL FORUM, SCENE OF HIS GREATEST TRIUMPHS.

20-year-old road roommate. "Good motivation for him to play with Lemieux, against Gretzky. He can bring back a lot of good stuff from the experience. The young guys on the team will be asking him questions. It could be a good motivation for the team, too."

Said Sakic: "It makes me feel good and bad that Guy got asked and didn't go. He had a good first half, and if he hadn't been injured [for 16 games],

I'm sure he would have gone. He's an incredible guy to watch and play with."

Nowhere was Lafleur more incredible to watch than in his return to the Montreal Forum, scene of his greatest triumphs. On January 9, 1990, Lafleur and the Nordiques renewed the Battle of Quebec by laying a 5-2 pasting on the Habs right in their own den.

Lafleur scored a goal at 8:12 of the first period that *Gazette* columnist Michael Farber described as a "highlight film" classic. Lafleur took a perfect pass from Michel Goulet on the power play and, from the top of the right circle, rifled a shot into the top right corner.

"[Montreal goalie] Brian Hayward had started to go down, but no matter — Lafleur's was a perfect shot, hard and rising and overwhelming," wrote Farber. It was Lafleur's fourth goal against the Habs while playing in an enemy sweater. His first three had come the previous season as a member of the New York Rangers.

After the game, he tried his best to seem nonchalant. "I was glad the goal came in a win, that it wasn't just a moral victory this time," he told reporters. "It was different playing the Canadiens this year and last. Now it was just a red uniform out there."

Of course, it's impossible that the Canadiens could ever be "just a red uniform" for Lafleur, not after all his history there. Even in his twilight years with another club — a provincial rival, no less — he was always at his best when the Habs were involved.

As Farber quipped in his column, "More than six years after his final game with the Canadiens, Guy Lafleur still is making a living off them."

95

HOCKEY
BITE
IN CANADA

GUY À LA CARTE
BY DAVE STUBBS

IT WAS MARCH 2003, and the Montreal Canadiens were a month away from missing the NHL playoffs for the fourth time in five seasons.

This was a futility unheard of in the history of the league's most successful franchise, and one that was not sitting well with Guy Lafleur, arguably the most thrilling player to ever wear the *flannel sacré*, as the Canadiens jersey is reverently known in Quebec. In a city and a province where Catholicism and the Canadiens are usually worshipped with equal passion — praise the Lord and *belle arrêt, Théo!* — the sentiment of the fans was disturbing. It wasn't so much devastation they felt as it was resignation and, worse, indifference. Lafleur sat in the mid-morning calm of the Mikes Signature restaurant he owns in Berthierville, Quebec, an establishment that bears his name and likeness on its outside sign. Around him, his staff was busy setting tables for the lunchtime rush. Just as he finished discussing the merits of adding a baked potato to his menu, he was asked an almost half-baked question: "So what do you make of your team?"

His smile splashed into his coffee mug and his eyes hardened. Lafleur pulled on his cigarette, exhaling smoke that curled around him in a blue cloud, a perfect mirror of his darkening mood. His business today might be his restaurant between Montreal and Quebec City, but the Canadiens are forever

ARENA SEATING: GUY IN THE LOBBY
OF HIS RESTAURANT.

HE LED HIS TEAM TO
STANLEY CUP VICTORY
FIVE TIMES AND REMAINS
THE CANADIENS' MOST
PROLIFIC SCORER OF ALL
TIME, TWO DECADES
AFTER HIS LAST GAME IN
THE "CH."

in his blood. Perhaps it might have been wiser to ask about his pasta.

"It's frustrating for me, seeing guys making millions of dollars who don't give 100 per cent every night," Lafleur said, measuring his words. "There's something missing, and I don't like to see that. I was always a proud player and I played for a proud team."

You didn't need a magnifying glass to read between his lines. Pride was a cornerstone in Guy Lafleur's 13 seasons with the Canadiens, during which he never missed the playoffs. He led his team to Stanley Cup victory five times and remains the Canadiens' most prolific scorer of all time, two decades after his last game in the "CH."

Lafleur's mood brightened and he pointed out a huge photograph on a wall — himself with fellow Canadiens legends Maurice "Rocket" Richard and Jean Beliveau. The Rocket was holding the Stanley Cup aloft and a light above the photo cast the sterling trophy in a golden, almost ghostly glow.

"Look at that, the Cup looks like it's on fire," said Lafleur, breaking into a broad grin. "Show that photo to the Canadiens, will you?" In Quebec he is known as *le démon blond*, and his words certainly raised hell when they appeared in print the next day. In the Canadiens' current Bell Centre home, an hour west of Lafleur's dining room, they sounded not unlike a cannon being fired in a telephone booth.

That night he was honoured by his club at a pregame, on-ice ceremony recognizing his role with the 1976-77 Canadiens; that team won the Stanley Cup, and Lafleur won the Conn Smythe Trophy as the most valuable player in the playoffs. The crowd stood and roared "Guy! Guy! Guy!" And while the Canadiens tapped their sticks on the boards in tribute, surely they weren't overjoyed by his stinging rebuke. But neither could they utter one reasonable word of dispute.

HAB-TO-HAB: LAFLEUR AND TEAMMATE LARRY ROBINSON.

Here is one of the wonderful things about Guy Lafleur: he has never been reluctant to speak his mind. Not during his illustrious playing days and certainly not in retirement, when he could easily avert his critical eye as a salaried ambassador for the team he still represents from coast to coast and abroad.

"The Canadiens have to realize that while it's nice to have an image, your product is on the ice, not in the boardroom," he said. "If you have a good product, you'll have a good image and you'll have success. But you can't win with just the image. Some people don't realize that or they don't want to hear it.

"If you don't have the product, forget it. It's like a restaurant: you can have the nicest restaurant in the world, but if your product is shit you won't have any customers."

Canadiens president Pierre Boivin calls Lafleur "one of the top four or five most important and influential players in the team's history." He admits he winces when he hears Lafleur's harsh words as they relate to today's team, but he also admits he'd expect nothing less from the man whose No. 10 hangs from the rafters of the Bell Centre.

"That's Guy's character and his style," Boivin said. "He's always spoken from the heart and called things as he sees them. He's always been upfront, honest and communicative, perhaps more so than others, and that's earned him a lot of fan affection. You never quite know what Guy's going to say, or when he's going to say it, but I'm not surprised by it. Frankly, if we tried to monitor or control or massage that, we'd be doing ourselves and our fans a huge disservice.

"Number one," Boivin said, laughing, "you don't try to influence Guy. And number two, we'd be trying to filter a very important connection to our fans and a whole generation. His words have a lot of weight, even if we don't always agree."

And so it is that Lafleur lives his life as he played hockey: on his own terms. He is busier in "retirement" than he was as a player. The Canadiens can call on him 15 days per season to represent the club at a variety of functions. He is a high-profile national spokesman for Pfizer Canada, the maker of Viagra, and he's heard all the stickhandling wisecracks as he speaks to demystify men's sexual health. He travels extensively as an ambassador for the industrial giant Siemens Canada, and is a huge draw in old-timers' charity hockey games across the country.

When he's not between airports you'll find Lafleur in his franchise restaurant, probably three days a week for 10- to 15-hour stretches, alongside his wife of 31 years, Lise, and their adult sons, Martin and Mark. He's proud to tell you that, at least in part because of his insistence, Mikes has added that baked potato to the chain's menu, along with another of his suggestions, grilled salmon with rice.

His customers call ahead to make sure he'll be in before they set out from Montreal or Quebec City. And he's a hands-on restaurateur. He talks with his cooks, makes sure the food is hot leaving the kitchen, debates the Canadiens games his patrons watch at the bar and mingles with his diners, signing hundreds of picture postcards and blinking back the flashes of many cameras.

Lafleur remains as radiant a star today as he was in his brilliant prime — perhaps bigger, as a reminder of happier days on Montreal's long-Cupless hockey landscape.

"When I played, I was very close to fans, to people in general," he said in explanation. "They respect that I always speak my mind, even when I'm not

right. I've almost never refused anything from the public, and they appreciate it. There's not the same connection between players and fans any more, it's a different mentality. It seems the teams are trying to protect the players. From what, I don't know."

In truth, the Flower has never really hung up his skates, even though he played his final NHL game in 1991. That was in the jersey of the Quebec Nordiques, a two-year stop in the provincial capital having followed one season in the sweater of the New York Rangers.

HERE IS ONE OF THE WONDERFUL THINGS ABOUT GUY LAFLEUR: HE HAS NEVER BEEN RELUCTANT TO SPEAK HIS MIND.

Of course, Canadiens fans have forgiven Lafleur that indiscretion, conveniently erasing those three seasons from their personal record books even if souvenirs of them are displayed in his restaurant. His greatness belongs to the game of hockey, but those most loyal to the *bleu, blanc et rouge* say he was, is and always will be a Canadien, the heart and soul of some of its most magnificent teams. To them, he is not to be shared.

Fans remind him of this every day, on city streets and backwater burgs everywhere in Quebec, and on a much grander stage. In the autumn of 2002, a spectacular tribute was paid to Lafleur in Montreal. It was attended by more than 2,000 guests, from legendary teammates to star struck fans; entertainers included some of the biggest names in Quebec show business, including singer Robert Charlebois and impersonator Andre-Philippe Gagnon, and the evening featured tributes taped by then prime minister Jean Chretien and Senator Frank Mahovlich. The production later aired on Quebec TV to huge ratings and then sold briskly on a two-disc DVD.

"WHEN BELIVEAU WOULD SCORE IT, YOU'D SAY, 'WHAT ELSE DID YOU EXPECT?' WHEN LAFLEUR WOULD SCORE IT, HE'D PULL YOU OUT OF YOUR SEAT. AND HE PULLED ME OUT OF MY SEAT MORE THAN ANY OTHER CANADIEN."

On a club that claims 41 players in the Hockey Hall of Fame, the Flower is in the pantheon of a front-line few who have transcended the game, whose talent and devotion to hockey have defined not merely a roster but an era. Rocket Richard might have been the Canadiens' most lethal weapon from the blue line to the net, and Beliveau might have been the team's most stately playmaker and silky goal scorer, but flying from one end of the rink to the other, Lafleur is likely the most electrifying player to ever wear the CH.

Red Fisher, senior hockey writer for the *Montreal Gazette*, covered every

season played by Beliveau and Lafleur, and from 1955 the final five years of Richard's career — "the Rocket's back nine," as he says.

"Lafleur didn't do what the Rocket could do, and that's carry people on his back," Fisher said. "Lafleur was too fast, too tricky, too creative. Both he and Jean Beliveau were winners, and they and the Rocket could all get you the big goal. When Beliveau would score it, you'd say, 'What else did you expect?' When Lafleur would score it, he'd pull you out of your seat. And he pulled me out of my seat more than any other Canadien."

Lafleur remains a refreshingly candid voice in a hockey world populated by those fluent in cliché. He will ruffle feathers and even shock the game's stiff-collared establishment almost every time he speaks on the subject. He has said the NHL would be a better league if a dozen teams were folded and a European division were created to showcase the different styles played on two continents.

He is saddened by the current product, its mind-numbing defensive trap and other robotic systems having stripped the game of the free-wheeling beauty he knew as a player. The Canadiens used to play firewagon hockey; today, Lafleur bemoans the missing spark.

"The people tell me, and a lot of the former players who are in the public, a lot of stuff. You get to a point when you're sick and tired of it," he said. "When you look at the games, you see they're right. The league has to make the game more spectacular so people will have more interest in watching it."

When told that NHL commissioner Gary Bettman sings the praises of the on-ice product, Lafleur suggested with brutal frankness: "Tell him to buy a team and he'll see how great it is." Then he added, with a laugh, "But I don't think he's going to buy one."

Virtually every tangible souvenir he has left of his stellar career is displayed in his restaurant. In the spring of 2001, he sold 120 remarkable pieces of memorabilia to an American auction house, from replica Stanley Cups and his Conn Smythe, Hart and Art Ross trophies to milestone pucks and jerseys and plaques. He kept for himself his Hall of Fame ring and some paintings, with other items for the restaurant, and two Stanley Cup rings for his sons.

"I can't bring everything with me when I die," he reasoned. "Financially, I didn't need to do it. But this stuff had been in boxes in my garage and basement, so I thought I might as well give fans and collectors a chance to share them. They're the ones who appreciate these things."

Of course, Guy Lafleur doesn't need these baubles to remind him of his place in hockey history. With every meal he serves and every autograph he signs, he has his countless fans to remind him of the days they saw le *démon blond* streaking down right wing, his windswept mane never quite catching up.

Dave Stubbs is a feature writer with the Montreal Gazette. *He was a 14-year-old Canadiens fan in 1971 when he clipped Guy Lafleur's draft-day photo out of the newspaper for which he now works.*

WHAT THEY SAID:
QUOTABLE
QUOTES
ON GUY LAFLEUR

"DO YOU LIKE GUY LAFLEUR? I LIKE HIM, TOO. IN THE WINTER, HE REPLACES THE SUN."
— SINGER ROBERT CHARLEBOIS TO THE CROWD AT MONTREAL'S OLYMPIC STADIUM

"HE'S NOT THE EASIEST PLAYER TO PLAY WITH, BECAUSE HE'S ALL OVER THE ICE. HE DOESN'T KNOW WHAT HE'S GOING TO DO, SO HOW CAN I KNOW?"
— MONTREAL LINEMATE STEVE SHUTT, ON LAFLEUR'S PENCHANT FOR IMPROVISATION

"IF IT WASN'T FOR THAT GUY, I'D HAVE A COUPLE OF STANLEY CUP RINGS TO WEAR."
— FORMER BOSTON COACH DON CHERRY

"HE IS CONSTANTLY BEING HAMMERED AND FOULED BUT HE NEVER LETS IT BOTHER HIM, NEVER TRIES TO RETALIATE AND JUST KEEPS ON GOING. IT'S AS IF HE'S SAYING, 'YOU WANT TO FOUL ME, WELL, THAT'S YOUR PROBLEM, NOT MINE.'"
— TEAMMATE LARRY ROBINSON, ON LAFLEUR'S LEGENDARY FOCUS

"HE LITERALLY MADE FOOLS OF US IN THE THIRD PERIOD. HE HAD WINGS AND WE COULDN'T STOP HIM."
— KANSAS CITY SCOUTS COACH BEP GUIDOLIN

"DID YOU EVER NOTICE THAT GUY DIDN'T SWEAT? HE SEEMS TO WALK ON A RED CARPET ALL THE TIME. NO. 10, THE FLOWER, THAT'S IT! HE'S IN THE GARDEN ALL BY HIMSELF."
— WASHINGTON CAPITALS DEFENCEMAN ROD LANGWAY PAYS TRIBUTE TO HIS FORMER HABS TEAMMATE

"BESIDES HIS ENORMOUS ABILITY AND GREAT DESIRE, GUY HAD EXTRAORDINARY CHARISMA, THE ABILITY TO BRING SPECTATORS TO THE RINK AND THEN SHOW THEM SOMETHING UNUSUAL."
— SCOTTY BOWMAN, LAFLEUR'S COACH FOR SEVEN YEARS WITH THE CANADIENS

"HE IS THE MOST 'GOAL-DANGEROUS' PLAYER I'VE EVER SEEN."
— BOSTON BRUINS GM HARRY SINDEN

"I'D GAMBLE AND MOVE OUT OF THE NET TO CHALLENGE JUST ABOUT ANY PLAYER IN THE LEAGUE. BUT LAFLEUR? NO WAY! WHEN YOU GUESS OR GAMBLE ON HIM YOU ARE GOING TO BE STANDING THERE LOOKING DUMB WHEN THE PUCK ENDS UP IN THE NET."
— WASHINGTON CAPITALS GOALIE AND FORMER LEAF MIKE PALMATEER

"HE CAN BEAT YOU ONE-ON-ONE ALMOST ANY TIME HE WANTS."
— BRUINS DEFENCEMAN BRAD PARK

"THE MOST COMPLETE PLAYER IN THE GAME TODAY."
— HABS GREAT JEAN BELIVEAU, PAYING THE ULTIMATE COMPLIMENT

"THE DIFFERENCE BETWEEN LAFLEUR AND ME IS THAT I USED TO SCORE ALL MY GOALS FROM CLOSE IN. GUY IS A MUCH BETTER STICKHANDLER THAN I WAS. THE REST OF HIS GAME RESEMBLES MINE."
— HABS LEGEND ROCKET RICHARD

"THEY TORE THE %@!$%& ROOF OFF THE PLACE."
— HABS COACH BOB BERRY, ACKNOWLEDGING HOSTILE FAN REACTION AFTER HIS DECISION TO BENCH LAFLEUR DURING THE 1983–84 SEASON

"HE DID EVERYTHING SO NATURALLY. THERE WAS NO NEED FOR A GAME PLAN WITH GUY. HE DID THINGS ON THE ICE THAT WE HAD NEVER SEEN BEFORE."
— LAFLEUR'S FORMER LINEMATE JACQUES LEMAIRE

"I FELT AS IF A LITTLE PIECE OF MYSELF DIED WHEN I HEARD THE NEWS."
— OLD RIVAL MARCEL DIONNE, COMMENTING ON LAFLEUR'S 1984 RETIREMENT

CAREER STATISTICS

GUY LAFLEUR

REGULAR SEASON QMJHL, NHL

YEAR	TEAM	GP	G	A	PTS	PIM
1969–70	**QUEBEC REMPARTS**	56	103	67	170	105
1970–71	**QUEBEC REMPARTS**	62	130	79	209	135
1971–72	**MONTREAL CANADIENS**	73	29	35	64	48
1972–73	**MONTREAL CANADIENS**	70	28	27	55	51
1973–74	**MONTREAL CANADIENS**	73	21	35	56	29
1974–75	**MONTREAL CANADIENS**	70	53	66	119	37
1975–76	**MONTREAL CANADIENS**	80	56	69	125	36
1976–77	**MONTREAL CANADIENS**	80	56	80	136	20
1977–78	**MONTREAL CANADIENS**	78	60	72	132	26
1978–79	**MONTREAL CANADIENS**	80	52	77	129	28
1979–80	**MONTREAL CANADIENS**	74	50	75	125	12
1980–81	**MONTREAL CANADIENS**	51	27	43	70	29
1981–82	**MONTREAL CANADIENS**	66	27	57	84	24
1982–83	**MONTREAL CANADIENS**	68	27	49	76	12
1983–84	**MONTREAL CANADIENS**	80	30	40	70	19
1984–85	**MONTREAL CANADIENS**	19	2	3	5	10
1988–89	**NEW YORK RANGERS**	67	18	27	45	12
1989–90	**QUEBEC NORDIQUES**	39	12	22	34	4
1990–91	**QUEBEC NORDIQUES**	59	12	16	28	2
NHL TOTALS		**1127**	**560**	**793**	**1353**	**399**
NHL PLAYOFF TOTALS		128	58	76	134	67

112

CAREER FACTS AND HIGHLIGHTS

BORN SEPTEMBER 20, 1951, IN THURSO, QUEBEC. RIGHT WING, SHOOTS RIGHT, 6' 0", 185 LBS.

NAMED TO THE QUEBEC JUNIOR HOCKEY LEAGUE FIRST ALL-STAR TEAM IN 1970 AND 1971 AS MEM-BER OF QUEBEC REMPARTS

MONTREAL CANADIENS' FIRST CHOICE, FIRST OVERALL, IN 1971 AMATEUR DRAFT

ENGLISH NICKNAME "THE FLOWER," A LITERAL TRANSLATION OF HIS SURNAME; FRENCH NICKNAME "LE DEMON BLOND"

WON FIVE STANLEY CUP CHAMPIONSHIPS WITH THE CANADIENS, INCLUDING FOUR IN A ROW

HAD SIX CONSECUTIVE 50-GOAL SEASONS, FROM 1974–75 TO 1979–80

NAMED TO THE NHL FIRST ALL-STAR TEAM SIX TIMES, FROM 1975 TO 1980

WON THE ART ROSS TROPHY, THE REGULAR-SEASON POINT-SCORING TITLE, IN 1976, 1977 AND 1978

WON THE LESTER B. PEARSON AWARD, AS THE LEAGUE'S OUTSTANDING PLAYER AS SELECTED BY THE NHL PLAYERS' ASSOCIATION, IN 1976, 1977 AND 1978

WON THE HART TROPHY, THE LEAGUE'S MOST-VALUABLE-PLAYER AWARD, IN 1977 AND 1978

WON THE CONN SMYTHE TROPHY, AS OUTSTANDING PLAYER IN THE PLAYOFFS, IN 1977

SCORED 560 GOALS AND 793 ASSISTS IN 1,126 NHL REGULAR-SEASON GAMES

SCORED 58 GOALS AND 76 ASSISTS IN 128 POSTSEASON GAMES

ELECTED TO HOCKEY HALL OF FAME IN 1988

HONOURED WITH A TROPHY, THE GUY LAFLEUR TROPHY, ANNUALLY GIVEN TO THE PLAYOFF MVP IN THE QUEBEC MAJOR JUNIOR HOCKEY LEAGUE

ACKNOWLEDGEMENTS

I would like to express my gratitude to Julia Kamula, the publisher of the *St. Catharines Standard* for furnishing rare photos from the 1971 junior series between Guy Lafleur's Quebec Remparts and Marcel Dionne's St. Catharines Black Hawks. Thanks also to Raincoast editor Derek Fairbridge for his guidance in helping build the Lafleur story arc, and to Bill Douglas, whose stylish layouts have enlivened the pages of all six books in this series.

Thanks also to contributors Mark Lepage, Dave Stubbs and Doug Herod, and especially to friend and former *Toronto Star* colleague Frank Orr, whose hockey know-how is exceeded only by his warmth, humour and generosity. Special thanks to George Hulme, who shared his memories of the young Guy Lafleur and to my dad, Daniel MacInnis, who took me to junior games as a kid and awakened in me a lifelong passion for the sport. Finally, a tip of the helmet to *Montreal Gazette* editor Lucinda Chodan for her friendly help and advice.

Archival photographs were kindly provided by Craig Campbell of the Hockey Hall of Fame and by Trish Desjardins of the *Montreal Gazette*.

ALSO AVAILABLE

REMEMBERING PHIL ESPOSITO

Craig MacInnis, Editor

When we think of Phil Esposito's greatness — his record-setting 76 goals in the 1970-71 NHL season; his heroic role in Team Canada's victory over the Soviets in the1972 Summit Series — much of it seems explained by his "ordinariness." Lacking the pure athleticism of Bobby Orr, or the dazzle of Bobby Hull, "Espo" got by on qualities that seem more in line with the values of the average person — a proud work ethic, a sense of humor and an unabashed desire to succeed. Maybe that's why we couldn't help but love him.

1-55192-639-3 $24.95 CDN • $16.95 US

RAINCOAST BOOKS
www.raincoast.com

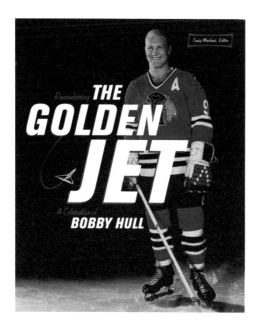

REMEMBERING THE GOLDEN JET

Craig MacInnis, Editor

His blistering slapshot revolutionized the game. He led what some argue was the best team in NHL history — the 1960–61 Chicago Black Hawks — to a Stanley Cup victory. He was the ultimate combination of power, speed and intimidation. Two decades after his retirement, Bobby Hull remains one of the most colourful characters in hockey, a high-flying icon in a game with few new superheroes. Here is a rare and compelling tribute to the man who transcended the game and touched hockey fans everywhere.

1-55192-633-4 $24.95 CDN • $16.95 US

RAINCOAST BOOKS
www.raincoast.com

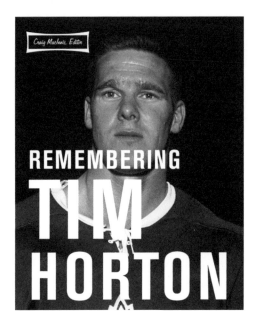

ALSO AVAILABLE

REMEMBERING TIM HORTON

Craig MacInnis, Editor

For 18 years, Tim Horton captained a stellar Toronto Maple Leaf defensive corps that featured fellow greats Allan Stanley, Bobby Baun and Carl Brewer. Horton, a constant threat to Bobby Hull and other offensive powerhouses of his day, led the Maple Leafs to four Stanley Cups in the 1960s, including the franchise's last Cup win in 1967. The powerful rear guard shared All-Star honours with Bobby Orr and Pierre Pilote, establishing him as one of the best defencemen ever.

1-55192-631-8 $24.95 CDN • $16.95 US

RAINCOAST BOOKS
www.raincoast.com

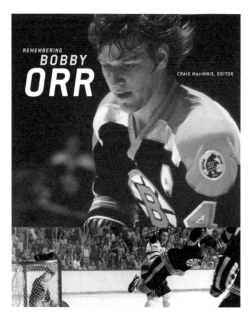

RAINCOAST BOOKS
www.raincoast.com

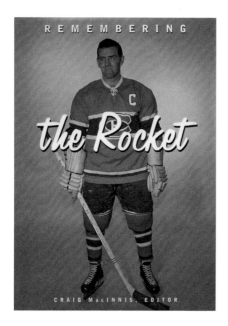

ALSO AVAILABLE

REMEMBERING THE ROCKET

Craig MacInnis, Editor

He has been called the "greatest goal scorer in professional hockey history," not least for his astonishing feat of notching 50 goals in 50 games. Yet that alone hardly explains his legend. Maurice Richard not only ushered in hockey's modern era with his prolific scoring touch and fiery play, he also came to symbolize the hopes and fears of an entire culture. Quebec in the 1940s and 1950s wanted a hero and they found one in Richard — a fierce competitor, a skilled athlete and a proud warrior.

1-55192-629-6 $24.95 CDN • $16.95 US

RAINCOAST BOOKS
www.raincoast.com